Are You Considering

Psychoanalysis?

Edited by **KAREN HORNEY**, M.D.

W · W · NORTON & COMPANY

New York · London

W. W. Norton & Company, Inc., 500 Fifth Avenue, New York, N.Y. 10110

ISBN 0-393-00131-8

W. W. Norton & Company, Inc. is also the publisher of the
works of Erik H. Erikson, Otto Fenichel, Karen Horney, Harry Stack
Sullivan, and The Standard Edition of the Complete Psychological
Works of Sigmund Freud.

Book Design by John Woodlock

PRINTED IN THE UNITED STATES OF AMERICA
4567890

Contents

Contents

Foreword

WHEN the Association for the Advancement of Psychoanalysis was founded in May, 1941, it defined community education in psychoanalysis as one of its aims. With that end in view, a group of interested laymen organized the Auxiliary Council for the Association in March, 1942.

Since that date, the Auxiliary Council has been sponsoring lectures in psychoanalysis for the laity. These lectures are conducted under the auspices of the Association and are given by recognized psychoanalysts all of whom are affiliated with the Association. The topics are chosen for their public interest and in response to a public need. One of these lecture series was entitled Are You Considering Psychoanalysis? The demand for this course, the audience attendance and response, and the numerous suggestions received that the lectures be made more generally available contributed to the decision to publish them in book form. At the suggestion of the contributors, it was agreed that royalties from this book be utilized for the furtherance of the purpose for which the Auxiliary Council was organized.

The basic premises underlying the thinking of all the contributors are essentially the same. This has given the book a unity in its fundamental approach. However, it is natural that each contributor brings to his interpretation of the basic tenets of the psychology here developed his own particular individuality. As a result, there is variation not only as to details of interpretation but also as to points of emphasis and of style. The book thus possesses the dual advantages of unity of approach and diversity of presentation.

The first editing was done jointly; after each of us had read all the chapters, we all got together to discuss the content of each chapter. The prevailing spirit during these joint editorial meetings was so co-operative that they remain in our memory as an unusually good human experience.

Dr. Horney was willing to assume the responsibility of being our chief editor. To this task she brought the wealth of her psychoanalytic knowledge, the experience she gained from writing four major works on psychoanalysis, and the welding influence of her personality.

Miss Dorothea Oppenheimer was our literary editor. We want to take this opportunity to thank her for her effective and co-operative efforts.

The contributors' task was made easier and given zest by the interest and suggestions of W. W. Norton. His encouragement and backing gave us a most favorable and agreeable start.   THE CONTRIBUTORS

Introduction

PEOPLE of our time and civilization are increasingly in need of psychological help. Also to an increasing degree they are aware of their need. They seek therapeutic help from psychiatrists, psychologists, social workers, ministers, and from books. Or they turn to religious and ethical movements, the leaders of which, convinced they have found a way for a more satisfactory life, are eager to point it out to others.

In their search for help, more and more people are turning to psychoanalysis. Some, without knowing much about it, grasp at the promise analysis holds and are ready to plunge into it blindly. As a rule, this is not harmful. A conscientious analyst will not attempt therapy unless he sees a reasonable chance of helping the patient. And while being analyzed, the patient gradually learns what analysis means and what it involves.

But, while not actually harmful, such lack of preparation for analysis is not desirable. The patient should be sufficiently informed about the process itself; he should know what he may expect from it and what is expected of him. Finally, he should have some understanding of the deeper meaning and the goals of analysis. The main purpose of this book is to prepare the patient for the three stages of the therapeutic process—before, during, and after analysis.

What do people want to know and what should they know before they decide to be analyzed? The authors of this book have pooled their findings—specific information sought by patients before analysis, questions asked after lectures and experience in treatment.

In the first place the patient wants to know whether he can be analyzed with some chances of success. Can analysis really do something about his drinking, his depressions? Or does he really need analysis? He may feel that if it were not for his eating spells or his fear of heights, he would be quite all right. Is this difficulty important enough to warrant a lengthy and incisive therapy? Usually he feels still more concerned if he does not suffer from any such grossly visible symptoms, but has "merely" a pervasive dissatisfaction with life, feels tense or diffusely inhibited, has intangible difficulties with the other sex or with people in general. And so, on the one hand, he worries about whether analysis can help him—particularly if his disturbances are of long standing. On the other hand, he feels he is not really ill and hence not justified in asking for help.

10

Another patient may be fairly clear about needing and wanting an analysis but has fears and doubts about the procedure and wishes to discuss them. Will analysis make him introspective and selfish? Does it stand for moral license? Does it interfere with artistic faculties? Will it disturb his marriage or religion? Will it so upset him that he cannot carry on with his job? Will it make him dependent on the analyst?

Again others have already decided to be analyzed but feel at a loss as to how to go about it. To whom should they go? Is it important that the analyst be a man or a woman? Is it important that the patient likes him? Does it make any practical difference in therapy whether the analyst adheres to this or that school of thought?

Finally, the patient wants to be informed about such practical issues as expenses, time, length of analysis. The last question usually cannot be answered precisely. But the patient should know the criteria upon which the length of an analysis depends.

In many instances, without knowing it, the patient needs more than factual information about the issues mentioned. His questions, his worries, his concerns may be greatly determined by his personal neurotic problem, by his specific fears, expectations, demands on himself, claims for special prerogatives, by his pessimistic view of himself and of life in general. The preliminary interview, then, may turn into a piece of analysis. And he may need this help before getting started.

In this book we have tried to clarify these issues. We have tried to give factual information, and where there

11

was no clear-cut answer to a question we have indicated criteria which should enable a person to evaluate the question on his own. We have also attempted to point out those unconscious factors that may render certain questions and worries more poignant than they actually are.

As to the nature of analytical work, we found less guidance in the way of questions raised. People are apparently curious about it but their notions are perhaps too vague for concrete inquiries. However, our experience with patients during analysis showed us the factors about which they usually lack clarity. By and large we had to decide what we believe is relevant to know. First of all, most patients are not prepared for having real work to do in analysis, because they secretly hope that relieving insights will automatically be theirs. Even though emotional factors that interfere with the patient's work on himself will have to be analyzed as they emerge, he should realize clearly from the beginning how much the length and outcome of the analysis depend on his initiative, productivity, and co-operation. So we describe at some length what the patient is expected to do in analysis. But he should know, too, what the analyst does and what kind of help the analyst can reasonably expect from him.

Last but not least, we have tried to convey an understanding of the meaning and the goals of analysis by raising the question: what should be achieved when analysis is terminated? This question, to our knowledge, has never been satisfactorily answered. Our answer follows from our belief that analysis is essentially one of the most valuable helps to our growth as human beings. This implies that analysis is not and cannot be limited to the time during which patient and analyst work together. It is a process that in the form of constructive scrutiny should go on as long as we live. Analysis does not aim at turning out a finished product. Rather, its purpose is achieved when the patient can proceed on his own. Methods of progress after analysis are indicated.

This book is mainly directed to those who consider analysis for themselves or for their friends or relatives. It will also, however, give to those who are seriously interested in analysis a clearer picture of its nature and its aim. We hope that it will help to dispel mysterious notions about analysis by removing unrealistic expectations of a magic cure. Many neurotic people may dislike having such hopes destroyed, but it is constructive for them to approach analysis in the sober spirit of expecting results only from actual labor done.

KAREN HORNEY

Why Psychoanalysis?

ALEXANDER REID MARTIN, M.D.

ONE OF the most significant and far-reaching cultural developments of our time has been the rapid growth of public interest in psychiatry and its offspring, psychoanalysis. Emotional and psychological factors are now more and more widely recognized and accepted as causes of disease and serious disability. This whole trend received its greatest impetus from the experiences of World War II. The induction process which screened and classified the nation's manhood gave us the first accurate estimate of the appalling waste of human potentialities resulting from emotional illness. The evidence furnished by the psychiatric services that efficiency, morale, and the capacity to wage war successfully depended as much upon emotional health as upon physical health has helped to integrate more closely psychiatry and psychoanalysis not only with medicine but with the social sciences and the humanities. The status of psychoanalysis, in particular, was greatly enhanced by the rapid and dramatic success achieved in the treatment of cases of so-called combat fatigue. These men were not analyzed but the rationale and method of their treatment was based almost entirely upon the experience and findings of psychoanalysis.

From the Surgeon General's Office came the staggering announcement that out of 4,650,000 men rejected at the induction level for all causes, 1,825,000 or 39 per cent were rejected because of some type of personality disorder. Despite this screening, 43 per cent of all medical discharges from the services were neuropsychiatric cases while another 20 per cent of all discharges had personality defects. A survey of our entire wartime population, conducted by the Surgeon General's Office, revealed that about 50 per cent of all people in the United States who seek medical help present primarily emotional difficulties, that is to say, some type of psychoneurotic reaction to the problems in their lives. To those who are thus manifestly disabled by emotional factors we have to add a large group of people whose emotional disability and crippling go unrecognized. If we also include those who end in mental hospitals or in suicide, we have some idea of the immensity of this whole social problem and the great need for increased understanding and help.

To the better understanding and prevention of these disorders psychoanalysis has a great contribution to make. There is little doubt that many of the disabilities can be prevented through the timely use of psychoanalytic insight in parent guidance and education and, fail-

16

ing this, can be greatly helped by psychoanalytic treatment. The mobilization of the nation's psychiatric and psychoanalytic resources and the extensive research necessitated by total war provided strong evidence that emotional conditions in family life rather than individual economic circumstances are responsible for initiating most of the personality disorders of our young men and women.

Psychoanalysis concerns itself with the subtle interplay and formative influence in every human relationship. It has helped to make it clear that each of us is a unique and integral part of society and has an indispensable contribution to make to the health of the social body. Accordingly the factors that produce psychoneurosis and personality disorders are part of everyday life for all of us and concern conditions for which we are or can be responsible.

Any medical discipline that enlists in the service of bettering the emotional conditions of living should be widely understood. Psychoanalysis has passed the experimental stage. It has become an accepted medical discipline and like all other medical disciplines is continually undergoing change and improvement. Gradually it is extending its sphere of influence in the medical and social sciences and in education and is widening its field of effective application.

Psychoanalysis would be even more widely accepted and effective today were it not for the fact that those people who are most in need of treatment are usually quite unaware of the real cause of their difficulties. You will

17

see in the course of this book how deep-seated, unconscious factors determine the feelings, attitudes, and patterns of behavior of the neurotic individual to the detriment of his personality. You will see how—unwittingly—he perpetuates his condition. Without being aware of it he practices the most amazing, paradoxical and intricate self-deceptions, rationalizations, and face-saving strategies. These not only obscure the real source and nature of his illness and the immense waste involved but blind him to his great need for help. Wherever there is reluctance to undertake analysis, where many justifications are put forward for postponement and delay, and where misconceptions persist, such unconscious processes can be suspected. This is particularly true of the person who remains adamant in his refusal to see the need for analysis or who appears to "protest too much."

Because of the unconscious elements in the neurotic individual that work against his best interests, it is very often some close associate who first recognizes the need for help of some kind. The family doctor, close relatives, or friends are in a position to enlist analytic help long before it would ever be considered by the patient. But they are unprepared for this role.

Hence, the person who does consider psychoanalysis for the alleviation of emotional or nervous conditions that have no determinable physical cause is often plied with suggestions such as these: "*You* don't have to go to an analyst—that's only for people who can't help themselves. All you need is a little will power. Try and snap out of it." Or "You're in a rut—what you need is a change, a new outlook on life." Or "Forget yourself; get your mind off yourself; take a vacation." Or "If you want to unburden yourself, go to your family doctor or your minister."

By reason of such advice—which in many instances gains the support of the family doctor—it too often happens that psychoanalysis is considered only after everything else has failed. Out of this situation comes the widely prevailing last-resort attitude toward psychoanalysis, one of the obstacles to its wider use. For it discourages consideration during the early phases of illness when analysis in all probability would be better able to demonstrate its value.

The great tragedy is that too many individuals suffer for years and pass through the hands of many doctors and friends before they finally consider analysis. A sensitive, psychologically astute associate or physician will very often note the indications for psychoanalysis before the patient can, or he will recognize an earlier and a different set of indications than those put forward by the patient.

Certain unconscious processes and conflicts involving the whole personality form the hidden central core of neurotic difficulties. They invariably cause a disturbance in functioning which may or may not reveal itself to anyone. It should be clearly understood, however, that the outward signs and symptoms of such a disturbance will give the individual no real indication of the nature of the unconscious determinants. In a great many instances neither the patient nor his associates recognize the rela-

19

tionship of the various signs and symptoms to his deeply disordered life.

This disturbance in functioning will always involve the total personality, but it may make itself felt or reveal itself only in one particular area of functioning. For instance, the difficulties may be evidenced mainly in human relationships as in irritability, marked shyness, inability to get along with others. They may be expressed in circumscribed fears such as fear of darkness, heights, closed spaces, etc. Or they may manifest themselves in excessive emotional responses to the external situation such as worrying, depressions, temper outbursts. Or the disturbance may be seemingly restricted to physical functions.

In many instances the disturbances are obvious to no one but the individual himself, and he may take great pains to conceal his difficulties from others. In this category are strong feelings of inadequacy or immaturity, popularly known as the inferiority complex, feelings of incapacity for work, difficulties in concentration, or an inability to enjoy anything. Often the patient has a sense of being cramped and unable to grow despite outward appearances of comfort, luxury, and leisure and there is a dissatisfaction that cannot be reconciled with the external picture. Other very common subjective symptoms, which the individual may keep to himself for many years, are feelings of stagnation, boredom, and a sort of emotional deadness. All these symptoms of dissatisfied and cramped functioning characterize unconscious ways of living that lend themselves readily to analysis. But here again the individual does not usually relate his difficulties to a disorder within himself. He may blame external conditions or, if he does blame himself, he does not have the true explanation. He is likely to seek extraneous relief in various forms before he considers analysis.

Alcohol and drugs are frequently sought by such people as means of blinding themselves to their difficulties and of hiding them from others. Such means, though intended as a relief from disturbance of function, actually result in further impairment of functioning and thus vicious circles are set in motion. Psychoanalysis is seldom sought in early alcoholism because there is very often a strong inclination to conceal the fact from others. The most difficult person to reach is the one who feels that his periodic alcoholism is an understandable and justifiable way of seeking relief from external stress. By this rationalization he successfully conceals from himself his real unconscious problem.

Unconscious processes can cause serious disturbance of organic and physiological functioning, involving for instance sleep, eating, and the sexual life. Some of these are obvious only to the individual—such as sleeplessness, fatigue, drowsiness, loss of appetite, uncontrollable eating or drinking, headaches, gastrointestinal disturbances, or dizziness. Other physical symptoms are obvious to others—such as profuse sweating, blushing, vomiting, stuttering, and twitching. In the absence of any organic disease, we must consider such symptoms as expressions of deeply hidden conflicts in human relations. Physicians in the psychosomatic field of psychiatry have

21

pointed out that unsuspected conflicts and emotional difficulties can give rise to disturbances of organic functions simulating most of the conditions listed in medical textbooks.

Contrary to general belief, hidden conflicts do not necessarily or invariably disturb sexual functioning. There is no doubt, however, that many of them first express themselves in the sexual life—for instance in excessive masturbation, frigidity, and impotence. Hence, all persistent sexual difficulties should be seen as local signals of deep-seated, extensive disorders involving the whole individual and all his relationships with others.

Adherence to Freudian psychology still leads a great majority of patients to believe that, regardless of the symptoms they present, the basic cause is always a sexual one. And analysis is sought with this in mind. It is now becoming increasingly clear that the great importance of sexuality in neuroses lies in the fact that the basic patterns and conflicts of life are often more clearly revealed and find more vivid expression in the sexual relationship than in any other; for here the most intense feelings and the closest human intimacy and contact are involved. However, although the pattern adopted for giving and receiving sexual gratification is very often the epitome of the whole integrated life pattern, it is never its determinant.

Homosexuality should be seen, like any other personality trait, merely as one expression of the individual's attempt to deal with hidden conflicts that affect his entire life. Here, in his sexual life, the individual presents

22

a local expression of a compromise with his hidden conflicts—a compromise that is subjectively valuable and satisfactory to him. The compulsive habitual pattern disclosed in sexual or intimate relationships with the same sex is, then, a localized manifestation of the individual's whole attitude toward life. The homosexual is unaware that original potentialities or resources are wasted, mortgaged, or lost in maintaining such a pattern. As long as he is perfectly satisfied, he will meet any suggestions that he consider analysis with scorn, contempt, and derision. When some dissatisfaction develops and he undertakes analysis of his homosexuality, success depends upon the nature of the whole neurotic structure, of which homosexuality is only one manifestation or symptom.

Finally, in a great number of cases, the individual does not suffer from any of the manifest disturbances that we have mentioned. Despite underlying neurotic conflicts, to all outward appearances he may function very well. Such people may be emulated and adored. They have managed to arrange their lives in such a way as to counterbalance and satisfy to some extent their conflicting neurotic needs. There is but one criterion by which their underlying disturbances can be detected—and this applies to all neuroses—namely the discrepancy between potentialities and actual achievement. In spite of successes in this or that field of endeavor, they are living below their original potential. Such people usually scorn analysis. The great difficulty lies in bringing them to a realization of the waste involved in their particular way of life.

Neurotic disturbances are often difficult to detect because people tend to deceive themselves by converting their compulsive attitudes toward life into virtues. We find negativistic defiance and contrariness hailed as rugged individualism and originality; reactive compliance, as loyalty. The inability to say no becomes unselfishness and kindness. The inability to take a stand on anything is seen as great tolerance and broadmindedness. The inability to concentrate, persevere, and sustain interest in any one thing is glorified as versatility. The fear of sexual intimacy is glorified as chastity. The whole picture is indicative of a delicate and precarious balance of conflicting and compulsive tendencies. The slightest departure from the habitual mode of life immediately arouses intense overreactions, feelings of anxiety, insecurity, and indecision. Often the individual does not at first see his extreme overreactions as at all disproportionate; he feels that they are completely justified. Such overreactions are usually first observed by close associates.

The individual's glorification of his compulsive attitudes blinds him to the real difficulties, quite obvious to others, in his relationships. So he does not see his own need for psychoanalysis.

The reader may ask at this point: granted that these personality difficulties exist and that they constitute a tremendous social problem, can psychoanalysis really do something about them?

24

I would prefer to proceed positively here and say what psychoanalysis is rather than what psychoanalysis is not, but there are certain popular misconceptions which should first be cleared up.

Many people regard psychoanalysis as a form of dissection of the psyche, a breaking-down process similar to chemical analysis. They think of it as a kind of research and diagnostic instrument that serves primarily to reveal certain unsuspected feelings and attitudes toward themselves and others. They believe that the analyst, having demonstrated the presence of such attitudes and feelings, proceeds to give advice and treatment and, in keeping with the basic premise, attempts to "synthesize" the individual. There are some physicians and psychiatrists who do proceed in this manner with the sincere conviction that they are practicing psychoanalysis. This is essentially misuse and misapplication of the whole method. Psychoanalysis originated as a therapeutic procedure and in proper hands it operates continually, from the very beginning, as a relieving process. The doctor does *not* "synthesize" the patient. Rather, as the patient comes to free himself from his neurotic entanglements, constructive forces within him are simultaneously set in motion that enable him to grow as a human being.

Analysis is not the kind of treatment one ordinarily associates with a doctor-patient relationship. A condition is treated, it is true, but it is not treated by a prescription, a formula, or a blueprint from the analyst. This must be understood very clearly, for many individuals expect the analyst to advise them, to tell them how to

25

lead their lives. The experienced analyst does not set out to do this. His intention is to help the patient, through increasing self-expression and gradual opening up, to see and to feel for himself the kind of life he is really leading, and the analyst hopes to develop in him the capacity and willingness to change. To the question "What should I do?" the analyst would be inclined to say "First let us find out all of what you *are* doing."

There is a common belief that psychoanalysis is analogous to confession, to the bringing out of certain experiences and behavior of which the patient is fully conscious, but which he has felt to be socially so unacceptable and blameworthy that he has never been able to reveal them to anyone. Many who feel this way will not see the need for psychoanalysis and will be inclined to say: "Why be psychoanalyzed? Just let go and confide in someone. Confession is good for the soul!"

Analysis, while interested in all the motives for and the value of confession, is in no sense a confessional procedure. Rather, as you will learn, it uses its various techniques for the primary purpose of self-revelation: to reveal determinants and derivatives of everyday conduct and feelings that the patient is unconsciously hiding from himself. Many of these hidden tendencies and feelings, which began quite consciously in childhood, persist as an unconsciously self-perpetuated part of everyday living although they are detrimental to growth and have only subjective value for the individual.

Nor is analysis a teaching procedure that strives to superimpose facts upon individuals. It tries, rather, to elicit thoughts, feelings, and the inner and outer experiences of everyday living of which we are unaware. It aims to remind rather than to inform; and in contrast to the customary advice to the unhappy to "try to forget," analysis will say "try to remember." It is primarily a procedure of enlightening, revealing, awakening. Psychoanalysis—in the vanguard of the search for truth about human beings—is essentially a process of education. But here "education" is conceived according to its original derivation and meaning, in the sense of *educere*, to lead or draw out.

Many individuals come to analysis with the impression that their getting well depends entirely upon remembering childhood experiences. However, analysis is never undertaken merely in order to bring forgotten memories into consciousness. The recall of unhappy experience—upon which Freud placed such great emphasis—while of considerable importance and a great aid in bringing about awareness of one's whole life is no longer the ultimate therapeutic objective. The major emphasis in the analytic method is no longer on the so-called genetic causes but rather on the immediate perpetuating causes. Therapy aims at bringing about greater and greater awareness of what is going on in the immediate present. It is the linking of the past with the present, the patient's awareness of how and why the past patterns are operating in the present, that leads to genuine insight.

To the question "Why psychoanalysis?" the analyst will say: "Because psychoanalysis is the first organized medical discipline to blaze a trail into the unknown, unexplored dark continent that constitutes all of man's life lying below the level of his consciousness. Because it can help man get in touch with the darker reaches of his life and learn the deeply hidden sources of his strength and weakness. Because analysis is the most effective means toward revealing and dissipating acquired unconscious conflicts and other factors responsible for personality difficulties and toward disclosing and releasing the original potentialities for creative and constructive living."

The question could be answered more simply: "In order to know yourself." With the recent development of a broader concept of self, the fundamental therapeutic dictum "Know thyself" has acquired greater significance and value. Now that we see self as a unique but integral part of the social body, we see that knowing thyself means knowing what is going on consciously and unconsciously between ourselves and others as well as what is going on inside ourselves.

While psychoanalysis deals with disturbances *inside* the individual, it is unique among medical therapies in its equal and constant concern with what goes on *between* individuals. It deals, much more than is generally realized, with the everyday problems of living with others.

Psychoanalysis seeks to improve the patient's awareness of what is going on in his present relationships with people and in his relationship with himself; to bring about awareness of those ways of living and feeling that are so habitual that they have been lost sight of. Con-

28

tinuous use is made of the whole analyst-patient relationship to assist the emergence into consciousness of habitual characteristics, tendencies, and feelings which, in the neurotic, are in serious conflict.

If we regard acquiring awareness as the main reason for analysis your next logical question will be: "But is awareness, in itself, sufficient? If I find out what kind of person I am, will I change? Will I get over my fears and anxieties? Will I become more constructive and creative?" To this we can say that it is only through the *struggling emotional process* of acquiring awareness, of facing emerging conflicts, attitudes and feelings through the medium of the patient's personal relationship with the analyst that he finds his strength and reaches for the first time a true evaluation of his real self, his real feelings, and his true potentialities for change and growth.

With increased awareness he will come to feel that many of his attitudes, standards, and feelings toward himself and others, which he has clung to as indispensable, are mutually incompatible, actually detrimental to his well-being and no longer essential. He will realize that he is deceiving himself and that his gains are illusory. His creative resources are seen to be mortgaged in maintaining his way of life and only hollow victories scored.

Analysis, like other branches of medicine, is mainly concerned with causes rather than with symptoms; but some important differences enter into this field. We must remember that in a great many instances the patient's symptoms represent his unconscious attempts at finding relief from and compensation for deeply disturbed feel-

29

ings: they are self-deceptive devices that help him to remain unaware of his conflicting tendencies. Therefore, though he asks to be rid of his symptoms, there is at the same time a real underlying fear that they will be taken away from him. Analysis does not try primarily and immediately to get rid of symptoms. Rather, it has a careful regard for them as significant and integral elements of the whole personality, a greater understanding of their protective purpose or unconscious function in the neurotic scheme, and a clear realization of what each symptom is trying to express and what it means and does to the patient.

It must be emphasized that the patient who manifests definite symptoms is in distress because a delicately balanced compromise of compulsive and incompatible elements—expressed, for instance, in some particular fixed pattern of living—has been upset or because he is unable to achieve such a compromise. When in difficult life situations these compromises fail to operate, many of the symptoms arise for which psychoanalysis is first considered: morbid apprehension, tension, anxiety, panic, the feeling that "everything is going to pieces." Under these circumstances the neurotic's world *is* going to pieces. He does not realize, however, that it is not worth saving. Consequently, most of these people, when they seek analysis, unconsciously want to restore the old balance and the old defensive patterns. They are "helped" by any therapy that advocates a return to normal or back to the old self policy. Unfortunately this kind of therapy prevails all too widely and is one way in which our culture unconsciously perpetuates neurotic patterns. This should be clearly recognized because many who seek analysis are unconsciously motivated by an impelling need to restore a pattern of living that never was helpful in the first place and that will inevitably break down again.

Thus we begin to see that even when psychoanalysis is sought there are unconscious tendencies to use the experience to serve neurotic needs and to keep deeply hidden conflicts from emerging into consciousness. One unconscious neurotic motive for being analyzed is a compulsive need for power. Analysis is then sought to gain influence over others, to read minds and foretell the future. The analyst is seen as a man of magic, and there is a desire to acquire through him a similar omnipotence. Such motives prevail in those people who intellectualize every human problem, who are always ready with explanations and interpretations of symptoms and mannerisms, and are always wishing to guide others.

Certain people undertake psychoanalysis because of an unconscious neurotic need for someone to protect and comfort them, upon whom they can become strongly dependent.

Still others who seek analysis have lived lives of habitual unquestioning obedience, loyalty, and obsequiousness. They do everything that is expected of them but give nothing of themselves. Unconsciously they behave in this way toward the analyst, and feel justified in expecting in return the miracle of cure—that is, a reward without expending any real active effort in the process.

31

Many patients enter analysis without any awareness of this expectation of miracles. Quite unconsciously a bargaining relationship with the analyst is set up in which the patient is compliant, submissive, docile. He will sacrifice a great deal; he will undergo hardship and deprivation—coming, for instance, at 7:30 every morning—during all of which he is unconsciously building up a tremendous claim on the analyst.

Where there are parents or relatives, a wife or a husband, advising and paying for the analysis, the patient may submit to the experience in a very co-operative manner and then, unconsciously, use the experience in various ways to humiliate, impoverish, or weaken the family, even endeavoring to use the analyst as an ally.

Many will present themselves for analysis with the idea—sometimes verbalized and sometimes not—of becoming defiantly independent of the family, and they too will unconsciously endeavor to use the analyst as an ally in the service of this purpose.

Fundamentally the neurotic does not really deceive himself, for he never develops any real sustained feeling of security. What disturbs him and what he dislikes in himself is his whole neurotic pattern of living, its precarious balance, its insufficiency, its demands, its hypocrisies and self-deceptions. Unless he becomes more aware and faces the unconscious conflicts so well concealed within his pattern of living, he remains the unconscious perpetuator of that pattern.

We can see here another way of describing the function of analysis—that is, to make the individual aware

32

of the philosophy of life he defends so strongly and re- gards so highly, aware of the emptiness and the waste involved in following and maintaining such a philosophy, and aware of the resources that are being so expended.

We must never lose sight of the fact that, although much of the individual's energy is mobilized to maintain his particular neurotic approach to life or to re-establish it, there is always a positive, active, creative element in him that is working toward genuine, healthy growth. In other words, the growth principle is constantly operat- ing. In earlier life the individual's symptoms and neu- rotic pattern of living were actually his first attempts to deal with his life problems so that healthy growth and self-expression could take place. Instead of aiding his constructive drive, a blind and insensitive culture rein- forced his neurotic pattern, and ultimately this was self- perpetuated. The analyst represents one individual so trained that he will not repeat the error of the patient's culture and unconsciously complement or supplement the patient's neurotic ways.

The greater the neurosis, the less the manifest picture of the individual is like that of the true man. The real individual is lost in a web of entanglements and neurotic conflicts with all their determinants and derivatives. With the analyst, he sets out to find himself.

It must be emphasized that the goal of analysis is not to uncover weaknesses. The process of revelation ulti- mately discloses a person's strength. Those elements which are thought of or felt as weaknesses are always secondary; they are the network, the entanglements, and

33

the defenses that hide and obscure the original basic strength and unique potentialities. Analysis liberates energy from its involvement in conflicting and wasteful patterns of living.

It is not sufficient that the patient seek analysis to become healthy. He must ask: "Healthy for what?" To that we might say: "Healthy for closer creative intercourse with others." The goal of analysis is to narrow the gulf between individuals, to bring about closer creative relationships, to bring about greater interdependence of living. And this becomes more and more feasible as the individual, through analysis, becomes aware of himself as a unique, integral part of the social body.

The patient's improvement in his relationship with others occurs simultaneously with an improvement in his relationship with himself. Freud was of the opinion that an instinctive and innate hostility prevents man from ever getting close to himself and to others. We cannot subscribe to this fatalistic theory. Psychoanalysis shows that man is prevented from maintaining his essential closeness to people and to reality, from becoming aware of his interdependence, not by instinctive, innate factors but by acquired neurotic elements. The hostility that Freud defined as instinctive is actually a defensive, reactive hostility. Far from operating in the service of self-preservation, such hostility, aggression, or destructiveness only serves to preserve illusions. Analysis seeks to reveal those attitudes and feelings and tendencies that prevent individuals from growing closer together, from recognizing their interdependence. It deals with those

34

neurotic elements that perpetuate detachment and isolation.

The old saying "familiarity breeds contempt" echoes the Freudian fatalism, but it is true only for those who are defensive, grandiose, with no real sense of humility. Familiarity certainly does reveal the weaknesses of man, but it also reveals his strengths. It reveals ugliness but, at the same time, beauty. Those who have the courage and the humility to open their eyes and to draw more closely to their limitations can at the same time—and only at the same time—see their real strength. Because analysis increases awareness, it reveals potentialities and genuine feelings and makes possible a true evaluation of one's assets and liabilities. "Love thy neighbor as thyself" becomes meaningful and applicable only as you come to "love thyself." You must first know yourself and accept yourself for what you are.

Unless you have a genuine warm affection for yourself and a self-regard based upon knowing yourself, you can have no affectionate regard for others. It is not a matter of loving some illusion of yourself. When there can be recognition and acceptance of your own frailties and limitations, then there can be acceptance of the frailties and limitations of others. The important point is that only by having the strength and the courage to open our eyes to the so-called unacceptable and ugly in ourselves and in others can there be any awareness of what is beautiful and sound.

These psychoanalytic principles received their strongest and most unquestionable substantiation from men

35

exposed to the grim realities of war. It was commonly recognized among soldiers that the best leaders in combat, as well as the most reliable ones, were those who feared the worst and hoped for the best—in other words, those who could admit that they were afraid, who had the strength to see and feel the worst features of reality in themselves and others, because at the same time they could also see and feel the best features of reality.

With a knowledge of one's worth, the sense of inadequacy, of shallowness, of emptiness—so characteristic of neurosis—is dissipated, and the individual feels free to give, and to give without expectation of a reward. A person who is aware of his basic strength needs no appeal to him to give. He has a greater capacity to feel—wholeheartedly, richly and deeply—because he feels strong enough to prevent his reactions from overwhelming and getting the better of him. Only with the courage and the strength to feel sadness and pain can there be any ability to feel real joy.

What Schools of Psychoanalysis Are There?

VALER BARBU, M.D.

THE WEALTH of the material with which psychoanalysis deals has necessitated the constant development of new concepts. The purpose of these concepts is to facilitate orientation and to promote focusing on specific problems. A review of the more fundamental concepts of psychoanalysis would seem desirable.

If you have already done some reading of psychoanalytic literature you will know that psychoanalysis was founded by Freud and that in the course of time various other schools of thought have developed. In this chapter I shall review briefly the theories of the most representative schools of psychoanalysis.

The fact that several different theories have emerged has not been detrimental, on the whole, to the progress of psychoanalysis, but has served rather as an incentive toward the development of a more comprehensive viewpoint. Furthermore, the differences are not merely of theoretical interest but are of practical importance also, because the therapist's approach is largely determined by the particular theory he holds.

Sigmund Freud, the founder of psychoanalysis, was for many years also its chief contributor. The early analytic theories were almost entirely his creation. In the course of time, several of his most important disciples left Freud, because of disagreement on theoretical issues, and founded their own schools. The more orthodox Freudians completely repudiated the ideas of these secessionists. In recent years, however, some of the most experienced analysts of the old school have also attempted a rather radical revision of the theoretical field of psychoanalysis, in an effort to make it capable of further development. The most outstanding of these is Karen Horney.

As a method of therapy, psychoanalysis is based on the principle of self-knowledge. It makes a particular study of the unconscious motivations and conflicts that stand in the way of the individual's fuller development as a person. Since these problems are rather universal, psychoanalysis offers help not only for the sick, but also for the relatively healthy, in the effort to achieve a fuller development.

Since we can devote only one chapter to the subject of schools, this presentation must be limited to the essential features of each theory. Adler, Rank, and Jung differ rather widely from Freud, as well as among themselves. Horney's approach, on the other hand, is a more direct outgrowth of Freudian psychoanalysis.

38

THE THEORETICAL CONCEPTS OF FREUD

In the 1880's and 90's, Freud observed patients suffering from major symptoms of hysteria and made the discovery that some of them were relieved of their symptoms if they could be helped to recall painful childhood experiences. He was also impressed by the fact that they were preoccupied chiefly with thoughts and feelings of a sexual nature. He drew the conclusion that the difficulties were caused by sexual frustration. He subsequently developed a theory of sexuality, the libido theory, which has remained the backbone of the orthodox Freudian approach.

According to Freud, the most important factor in determining the growth of the personality is the sexual development. However, in his theory the concept of sexuality has acquired a very broad meaning, so that it has become synonymous with love as well as with pleasure-seeking of any kind.

Freud ascribed great importance to the libido, which he defined as the energy of the sexual instinct as represented in the mind.

At the most primitive stage of development, the as yet undifferentiated libido is thought to be invested in one's own body. This is the stage of narcissism in which the infant is supposed to be in love, as it were, with himself. Freud assumed that during the first five or six years of life the individual has to go through a basic sexual development in the course of which the libido undergoes some predetermined transformations, characterized by

39

certain phases. This development is made possible by the availability of a certain amount of love and is interfered with by deprivation of love or by traumatic or upsetting experiences which the child cannot handle emotionally or which have the meaning of deprivation of love.

The foundations of sexuality are laid in early childhood. The earliest expression of sexuality occurs in connection with certain zones of the body—the oral, anal, and genital zones respectively. These are invested with pleasure and their specific physical functions become particularly important to the child at a certain period in his development.

Freud maintained that each zone has a corresponding kind of libido, and he therefore called these areas erogenous zones. Accordingly, three main varieties of libido are postulated—the oral, anal, and genital libido. The oral and the anal represent earlier and more primitive forms of libido and they later merge into the genital libido.

The function of a particular erogenous zone occupies the center of the stage at a given period of early childhood and characterizes that particular phase. Because of the biological instinctive nature of the libido, the phases are considered inevitable. Freud assumed that activities connected with a certain zone satisfy not only important bodily needs but specific psychological needs as well and that they serve as a basis for the development of certain character traits. Rather complex personality traits are thus considered to be derivatives of certain

40

forms of libido. Insatiability and the desire to exploit are derived from oral libido; orderliness, hoarding, obstinacy, sadism are considered anal character traits; capacity to love is correlated with the genital stage. These traits are considered to be constituents of the oral, anal, or genital "character" respectively.

The genital zone becomes more important as the child gets involved in the so-called Oedipus complex. He wants sexual union with the parent of the opposite sex and is jealous and harbors death wishes toward the parent of the same sex. The Oedipus complex is not thought of merely as a product of a certain life situation of the child but as a biological necessity, a phase to which the human being is predestined by nature. The Oedipus complex in the boy involves the castration complex, that is, the fear of retaliation by punishment on the offending organ and the wish to protect oneself by passivity. Freudian analysis considers the Oedipus complex to be the nucleus of every neurosis. The little girl goes through a similar development with the difference that, not having a penis, she has to compensate for this defect by phantasying that originally she did have one, but that it was cut off as punishment for her sexual desires. It was cut off by her natural rival, the mother. She harbors an intense conscious or unconscious envy of a penis. Feminine psychology, according to Freud, inevitably bears the mark of what he termed "penis envy."

In order to get from one phase to another one has to graduate, as it were, from the preceding one. Freud conceived of the libido in strictly quantitative terms, in analogy with the principles of conservation and transformation of energy in physics. Therefore if much libidinal energy is tied down by fixation, for instance on the oral zone, there is little left for the anal or genital zone and for activities considered to be derived from these forms of libido.

If, as a result of traumatic experiences, a considerable amount of libido becomes fixated at one or several zones, this will interfere with the individual's development and will result in neurosis. Symptoms may not break out until later in life when, under the influence of emotional strain, great quantities of libido are thrown back to the fixation points. This process is called regression. Freud attempted to explain the differences between the various neuroses and psychoses according to the amounts of libido that were fixated at the oral, anal, or genital level respectively.

Freud assumed that the task of therapy is to release the dammed-up libido, and thus help the neurotic to avail himself of this energy. As a result of therapy, the libido is set free to follow its course as prescribed by its instinctive nature.

In a later period, Freud came to distinguish two basic instincts in man—the eros, or life instinct, and the death instinct. The life instinct includes all forms of the libido and represents the life-promoting tendencies. It is opposed by the death instinct which is destructive and represents the wish to return to the inorganic state.

The theory of the death instinct reveals a rather pessimistic view of human nature, according to which man is predestined by his instinctive nature either to hurt

42

himself or to direct this tendency toward others in some form of destructiveness, which may take a collective expression in such a phenomenon as war.

As he further developed his theory Freud came to consider the personality as being constituted by three parts, all of them partly or largely unconscious: the id, the ego, and the superego. The id is the instinctual libido reservoir. The ego is the part that makes contact with the external world. The superego is built on the basis of parental prohibitions and represents the internalized parental authority, the voice of the parent in oneself. The superego is endowed with self-destructive forces which Freud also considered to be instinctual in nature and derived from the death instinct.

In the light of the Freudian theory, the ego appears as a mere battleground of the other two forces which pull the individual in opposite directions. The ego is forced to develop various mechanisms with which to protect itself from being overrun by the inimical forces of the id and the superego. These defense mechanisms are aimed at evading the repressed strivings or at denying their true nature. Repression is considered the most important defense mechanism in neurosis. It is an unconscious process and is caused by conflict. What Freud usually meant by repression was the active keeping out of consciousness of the id strivings, the sexual strivings that are prohibited by the superego. The ego was later thought of as having to make a synthesis between the superego and the id.

An important variety of defense is the reaction forma-

43

tion. In defense against his sadism, for instance, a person may develop a reaction formation in which opposite tendencies are displayed, such as a drive to be excessively kind. Such defense mechanisms are mere make-shifts and the repressed forces continue to operate in the unconscious or to manifest themselves in disguised ways. The character of the person was then conceived of as being constituted chiefly of such reaction formations.

In order to mobilize the fixated libido, Freud thought it most important that in analysis one should strive to recover the earliest memories related to infantile sexual wishes. He believed that the neurosis is maintained mainly by the continuous pressure of these prohibited infantile wishes, because of which the neurotic must suffer from guilt and from symptoms that represent sexual gratifications. Accordingly it is necessary that in analysis the patient relive the so-called infantile libido situations.

In analysis the repressed strivings are gradually brought to consciousness and since Freud thought of them as primarily erotic wishes directed toward the parents, he saw them as being automatically directed toward the person of the analyst. This process Freud called *transference*. The patient places the analyst in the role of father or mother. By transference the libido is detached from the objects to which it was fixated on an infantile level and is transferred to the analyst and thereby made available for the ego's more mature use. Transference love in analysis is supposed to be the force through which the patient changes.

In analysis, according to Freud, the neurotic individual is under constant inner compulsion to repeat the vicissitudes of the sexual instinct which demands gratification. During analysis the oral, anal, and genital phases come up and are permitted a freer flow toward the resolution of the Oedipus complex. Freudian analysis is focused on this process. It is also necessary that the superego be reduced in intensity and that the individual relinquish enough narcissism to make his libido available for normal sexual relations. Through analysis the conflict between the id and the superego is diminished and the ego is thereby strengthened.

Freud devised a specific method for obtaining the material for analysis. This is the *free association technique* —a most valuable tool. The patient is instructed to say everything that comes to his mind, regardless of whether it appears important or unimportant, rational or irrational. Psychoanalysts still adhere to this fundamental rule. It leads to the uncovering of most important material, which is then discussed and interpreted.

Dreams were found by Freud to furnish excellent material for free association. He believed that dreams represent disguised fulfillments of unacceptable and therefore repressed unconscious sexual wishes. Dreams reveal the working of the unconscious. Freud worked out a method by which to interpret the distortions and the symbolic meaning contained in dreams.

Freud found the following limitations to analysis: the instincts may be constitutionally too strong; the individual may be too narcistic; a specific limitation—in men, too strong resistance to the recognition of passive homosexuality and, in women, refusal to give up the penis envy.

Freud's concept of human nature emphasizes what he thought of as instinctive needs. According to Freud, human psychology is governed ultimately by these biological forces. In the old Freudian type of analysis the analyst is very passive. The main focus is on the analysis of the libido and the rest of the personality is expected to take care of itself.

Many of Freud's observations have a sound basis and have been epoch making. Many of his theoretical formulations, on the other hand, have been misleading and in the course of time a radical revision became necessary. It is my belief that such revision has been made successfully only by Karen Horney.

It was Freud who found that neurotic difficulties begin in childhood. He called our attention to the importance of sexuality in human life and was a pioneer in fighting the secrecy and hypocrisy with which the subject was surrounded at the time of his early work. He discovered that we are influenced by irrational emotional forces to a much larger extent than we like to believe; that the neurotic actively resists facing some of the emotional forces which drive him; that these forces are powerful and that as a result of repression they operate largely unconsciously; that they appear in many forms; that these forms can be recognized by methodical procedure; that they are interrelated in terms of content as well as in their energetic or dynamic aspect.

However, he made some unwarranted assumptions.

Among them is the supposition that neurotic difficulties are basically instinctive and preponderantly sexual in nature and that the unconscious emotional forces which drive the healthy and the neurotic, the child and the adult are mainly certain varieties of the sexual instinct. His extension of the concept of sexuality is entirely unwarranted and has led to a disastrous confusion of thinking in regard to the fundamentals of human nature and, more specifically, to a one-sided emphasis on sexuality in the psychology of early childhood. The assumption that the basic problems of the adult neurotic revolve around unresolved infantile sexuality and that consequently the analysis of the adult neurotic should deal chiefly with the vicissitudes of infantile sexuality is unjustifiable. Even though the life of the child is naturally merged into sensuality to a much larger extent than the life of the adult, the neurotic child's basic problems are not exclusively of a sexual nature and therefore even a child's analysis should not focus on sexuality to the exclusion of other aspects of his development.

Freud's emphasis and extension of sexuality, it must be admitted, allowed him to cover a large area of the inner life of man and it gave him a tool with which to engage the neurotic's interest in himself—by tempting him to do it in his own neurotic terminology, as it were. Nevertheless, it also enabled Freud to avoid tackling our ethical conflicts. A therapist equipped with such a tool will not run the risk of being accused of trying to moralize to the patient, but he will also leave some of the patient's basic problems untouched.

47

Finally, Freud's theory that feminine psychology is governed by penis envy and his assumption of a basic death instinct in man are probably erroneous and bar the way to an effective therapy.

ALFRED ADLER'S INDIVIDUAL PSYCHOLOGY

Adler was a collaborator of Freud who parted from him about 1910. At first he conceived of the neurotic individual as one who constantly strives for superiority in order to compensate for some organic inferiority. Later he put less emphasis on organ inferiority and took a more thoroughgoing psychological view.

Owing to unfavorable constitutional and social factors, the individual who is headed toward a neurotic development is deeply impressed by his weakness and helplessness. In order to overcome his feeling of inferiority and to hide it from himself and others, he develops a drive toward superiority. The only healthy solution that is possible for him is to develop social feeling. In treatment, he must be shown that he is following an impossible goal. He is shown the way toward integration with society.

In evaluating an individual we must find out the relative strength of his need to dominate and the strength of his social feeling. The greater the latter in proportion to the former, the more valuable the personality.

Two conditions are essential to the healthy mental growth of a child: he must have healthy organs and he must have an opportunity to develop social feeling. In our society a child with inferior organs is at great disadvantage. He is made to feel inadequate as a person. He will easily develop a hostile and domineering attitude toward his environment. He may show this in an aggressive way; he may disguise it by adopting a submissive attitude. As he grows up, such an individual tends to become more or less isolated from society. This faulty basic attitude tends to persist through life.

Every child has feelings of inferiority, but he can gradually overcome them through social feeling. The essential task of upbringing is to enable him to achieve this development. Persistence of a feeling of inferiority would prevent such development. Compensatory strivings for power would similarly lead to a thwarted growth. Other people in the child's environment, particularly his parents, may help or hinder his growth as a person. They may help his development by guiding him toward social goals. They may hinder it by stressing the child's inferiority and by expressing contempt for him, or by inciting him to excessive ambition at the expense of social feeling.

The unconscious, to Adler, is that which the individual does not wish to know about, so as not to have to take responsibility for it. The more responsible the individual is, the larger his sphere of consciousness and the less his need of an unconscious.

A single psychological phenomenon—for instance, an attitude or a sample of behavior—cannot therefore be understood in isolation but only in the broader context of the personality. The most important context for Adler

49

is the unconscious striving for superiority. The key to psychopathology is to correlate the particular phenomenon with the secret goal of the individual. Therapy consists in enabling him to develop the healthy goal of social usefulness.

Adler believed that he could explain all neurotic phenomena by this single principle of the inferiority complex. He was the first to depart from the libido theory. Unfortunately, he also discarded some of the more valuable parts of the Freudian method. He made little use of the free association technique and deprived himself of the opportunity of working through his patient's problems in detail. Although there is much truth in it, his approach seems rather crude and his theory one-sided.

OTTO RANK'S WILL THERAPY

Rank's book by this title appeared in an English translation in 1936. He objected to Freudian analysis on the ground that it aimed toward changing the neurotic person into an ill-defined, formless, average type. In contrast, Rank believed that the neurotic had more in common with the creative. He spoke of both as "the strong willed," with the difference that the will of the creative is affirmative and that of the neurotic is negative.

A lifelong student of cultural history and of the psychology of religion and art, Rank considered the creative tendency as the essentially human quality. Man's creativeness is bound up with his spiritual strivings and found its earliest expression in religion. There his creativeness was projected upon supernatural beings. In his gods, man could worship his own wish and phantasy of greatness. Since this was a projected force and therefore beyond his control, he also dreaded it and had to placate it continually. Man's belief in immortality, which is expressed in religion, is not based merely on the awareness or the fear of death but more fundamentally it is an expression of his need to grow and to expand as a person. Man projected his own ideal self upon the gods and expressed his aspirations in art and religion. In the course of time he became more conscious of the meaning of his illusions, and he is now beginning to realize that his chief problem is what he wants to make of himself.

The neurotic according to Rank is a person who can no longer project his needs on God as historical man did. At the same time, because of conflict, he is unable to live up to his aspirations and will therefore deny them. Because of this denial of his will, he suffers from a continuous feeling of guilt. By will, Rank means the will to be oneself and the capacity to use one's irrational forces creatively. In therapy the neurotic should learn to recognize his will and to take responsibility for it.

The neurotic and the artist are the most individualistic people of our time. The will necessarily means asserting oneself as an individual and this implies wanting to be different. In order to become a distinct entity, one must develop the capacity to stand on one's own ground and to separate. Denial of this tendency results in the need to unite, to love. Freud took the neurotic need for love at its face value, but to Rank it was reactive and not genuine.

Man needs something to believe in. This is what he calls the truth. Rank said that the neurotic knows too much truth and that what he needs is illusions. He spoke of religion, art, philosophy, and love as "the great spontaneous psychotherapies of man," the therapeutic value of which lies in the fact that through them man can use his illusions creatively.

Rank's critics considered this a cynical standpoint because of its suggested implication that mankind must live on illusions. But viewed in the perspective of history, the beliefs of mankind, which were always supposedly based on truth, have continually changed and thus what people believe in is evidently not the objective, final truth. The truth is something provisional, something to be developed. But one has to have faith. Rank emphasized the need for faith in oneself and in one's own truth. This includes the need to develop one's own ethical standards. However, Rank took for granted the need for illusions.

From Rank's standpoint, Freud's therapy is biological because it is centered on instinct; Adler's is social because it sets out to align the individual with society. He considered his own truly psychological because it is individual centered. It emphasizes the will of the individual, which is the essence of his psyche. To Rank, the individual is his own creator. Therapy is not a matter of biology or sociology but of psychology, and it works by providing in the analytical situation a controlled experience that may lead to the development of faith in one's individuality.

The weakness of the Rankian method lies in its inadequate character analysis. Rank's therapy, like Adler's, is an attempt to solve neurotic difficulties by the application of one principle.

CARL GUSTAV JUNG'S ANALYTICAL PSYCHOLOGY

The chief cause of neurotic disturbances, according to Jung, is the failure to live according to the laws of the soul. In his numerous writings Jung has worked out and formulated in detail his own system of the structure of the psyche. The laws of the psyche are considered given by its own nature, and they are conceived as universal and eternal. The task of therapy coincides with that of wisdom; it is to make it possible to learn to live according to these inner laws. The internal harmony is made possible by the balance between the conscious and the unconscious. The true way of life is to live according to the order that reigns in the unconscious.

The structure of the psyche consists largely of pairs of opposites, such as thinking and feeling, sensation and intuition, as four varieties of function, and extraversion and introversion as two basic attitudes. Difficulties arise when one of these modes is overemphasized to the detriment of its opposite. Similarly, the conscious and the unconscious are thought of as complementary.

Parts of the personality may be split off and continue

53

an autonomous existence, of which the individual is not aware. These are called complexes. Symptoms, such as slips of the tongue, may indicate their existence. Jung agrees with Freud that these complexes are often the result of traumatic experiences. Years ago, Jung devised the association experiment for the detection of complexes.

Later, however, Jung derived his understanding of the unconscious chiefly from a study of the symbolism contained in all mythologies and, more particularly, in the ancient Eastern religious systems and from similar symbols he found in dreams. Whereas Freudian dream interpretation emphasizes the repressed sexual wishes, Jung sees dream symbols as the expression of timeless patterns of the unconscious. The personal unconscious is determined by the universal collective unconscious, and the patterns of the latter are called the archetypes. Examples of archetypal images are the mother, the father, the hero, the virgin birth, the rebirth, paradise, the wise man, the snake, the fish, the Sphinx, the world tree, etc. Their number is limited, and they stand for typical and fundamental human experiences.

The social façade—called the "persona"—may take on a rigidity that leads to a suppression of the deeper unconscious. The darker side of our personality—the "shadow" —causes difficulty because of our tendency to disavow it and to project it upon others. It is necessary that we allocate it where it belongs—in ourselves. Certain typical unconscious content refers to the experiences characteristic of the opposite sex, and such content is sup-

54

posed to be active in everyone. It is termed *anima* in men and *animus* in women. In working toward the development of one's real self, the persona, the shadow, the animus or anima must be thoroughly understood and their content be brought into harmony with the deeper levels of the collective unconscious. The same working through is necessary with regard to the so-called personal unconscious.

Suppression and neglect of the unconscious leads to the conscious being overflooded by the unconscious in a chaotic way. Such a state of regression constitutes, however, at the same time, a challenge to bring oneself into harmony with the unconscious. This can be facilitated through therapy. Therapy does not create a new order; it merely brings about more favorable conditions for the predetermined order of the unconscious to establish itself.

Jung strives toward a formal clarity and precision such as obtains in theoretical physics. He believes that it is particularly the man of Western civilization who needs outside help to square himself with the unconscious, because he has become estranged from it to an unusual degree.

While all schools agree in regarding the neurotic as a person whose inner balance is disturbed, each considers him from a different angle, and consequently each offers a different remedy. With Freud the emphasis is on the difficulties of the sexual development; with Adler it is the overcoming of the egocentric inferiority-superiority drive by adjustment to society; with Rank it is the establishment of the uniqueness and independence of the individual through creativeness and assertion of his own will; for Jung it is a problem of getting oneself in harmony with the inner structure of the soul—which is conceived in terms supposedly valid for all times and places.

What Jung offers is akin to a religious solution. His system may be regarded as an attempt at devising a universal scientific religion. It is probable that at the present time, at any rate, only a few selected individuals would respond to this method.

New developments in psychoanalysis that took place in the 1930's are associated with the names of Harry Stack Sullivan, Erich Fromm, and Karen Horney. It is characteristic of all three that they abandoned Freud's one-sided orientation resulting from his strict adherence to the libido theory but that they preserved, on the whole, many of his other basic formulations.

In the course of intensive psychiatric work in mental institutions, Sullivan found that the development of the individual's insight into his relationship with other people was an essential factor in therapy. In consequence, sexuality was seen as only a part of the larger scheme of human relationship. Erich Fromm is not a medical man but a sociologist and a psychoanalyst, and with this unusual combination of knowledge he saw more clearly than most the influence of the social-economic factors on character development. His findings indicated that neurotic difficulties were not fixed biological developments but potentially plastic psychological reactions.

KAREN HORNEY'S THEORY OF PSYCHOANALYSIS

Karen Horney has been largely responsible for the development in recent years of a more progressive type of psychoanalysis. She has presented her views on neurosis clearly and consistently in several books. Her theory will be taken up in the following chapter. I shall here attempt only to indicate how Horney's approach differs in spirit from Freudian analysis.

We must try to see Freud in the perspective of his time. The late nineteenth century was predominantly materialistic and cynical in its thinking. This was partly due to the astounding advances made in the sciences: the progress of physics and chemistry, the discovery of germs as causes of diseases, the progress of pathology and, finally, Darwin's theory of the evolution of man from the animal. The animal nature of man was stressed. Something had to be found in his animal nature to account for his difficulties as a human being. Parts were made to account for the whole. Sexuality appeared to Freud as the foundation of personality and character. Specialization was glorified; larger horizons were lost sight of. Freud's theories fit very well into this so-called scientific period.

Gradually medical men themselves became aware of the dangers of specialization and isolation from other branches of knowledge, especially those of sociology and the humanities, and they began to show an interest in a broader viewpoint. This was in keeping with progress in the field of philosophy, in which a better understanding of the relationship of parts to the whole was achieved. The importance of grasping the meaning of larger structures became more and more evident. In the field of psychoanalysis this viewpoint led to a re-examination of the meaning of sexuality. In the place of the Freudian formula, according to which character is determined by sexuality, it was found that sexuality was largely determined by character.

Horney's theory is an expression of this development. Therapy, according to her, involves the understanding of the whole neurotic character structure. The healthy person has a certain strength, unity, and capacity of self-determination. Everyone has the inherent capacity to develop into such a person. In the neurotic individual this development has been interfered with. The growth of a personality is largely determined by the kind of relationships developed with other people. Neurotic development is the consequence of disturbed human relationships, and the neurotic structure perpetuates the disturbed relationships with people.

Analysis as seen by Horney offers a human relationship that is realistically secure and in which one has an opportunity to bring the neurotic devices out into the open, to see them as part of oneself, and to take an interest in modifying them. In place of neurotic solutions of problems, one can acquire reasonable ways of dealing

58

with oneself and with others. Through one's own effort one finds a way to win back one's birthright, confidence in one's own resources, and self-esteem based on belief in values one can live up to.

Although Horney rejects the libido theory, she may be considered a follower of Freud. Like Freud, she believes that the chief task of psychoanalysis is the study of unconscious motivations. In analysis she makes consistent use of the Freudian technique of free association. The important difference is that in place of the analysis of the libido she puts analysis of all the unconscious components of the character. There is no minimizing of the neurotic difficulties. One has to deal with them in all their complexity. The neurotic attitudes are comparable in their strength, pervasiveness, and consistency to philosophies of life. Although largely unconscious, they are defended with great energy and tenacity. In consequence, the individual suffers great emotional loss and may entertain feelings of hopelessness.

Nevertheless, in contrast with Freud, Horney's outlook is definitely optimistic. There is no need to assume a basic destructiveness in human nature. The fuller understanding of the neurotic structures also opens better ways by which the neurotic conflicts can be resolved. Therapy should set free the individual's inherent capacity to grow into a wholesome human being.

What Is a Neurosis?

MURIEL IVIMEY, M.D.

WE HAVE given you a general review of the different schools of psychoanalysis, ending with a brief section on the theories developed by Karen Horney. In this chapter I shall discuss her point of view in some further detail. I shall deal with what is fundamentally important in neurosis in order that you may get a general understanding of its manifold difficulties, its various manifestations, and its innumerable symptoms. My main focus will be on the total character of the neurotic personality from which these difficulties arise rather than on the manifestations or symptoms themselves. This theory of neurosis is the basis of discussion in the ensuing chapters.

Theory is an essential tool in scientific work. It is not to be confused with guesswork or speculation or pure abstraction. It is a rational and logical attempt to explain and correlate as many of the observed phenomena as possible at a given period in the development of a science. Since no theory is ever perfect, sooner or later weaknesses and false concepts come to light. Then scientists modify and revise their theory. When experience reveals evidence that calls for radical changes, an entirely new approach to scientific problems becomes necessary. Sometimes people feel uneasy or skeptical about a new theory for it means that they must abandon accustomed ways of thinking. However, many who have had their own doubts about the validity of existing concepts are willing and eager to learn of progress in theory that offers greater benefits to mankind in the practical application of a science.

Our new theory brings into sharp and unequivocal focus the psychic life of man—his entity as a person. We believe that psychic being or personality has its own unique essence and directives, its own forces for survival, its own dynamics of development and growth, and its own internal and external fulfillment. Its development and growth can be interfered with; it can become sick, inhibited, and distorted. Neurosis is the expression of this kind of development. With this focus a psychology emerges clear and distinct, unconfused with issues relating to organic instinctual considerations as basic factors in attempting to understand man's nature, sick or well.

This frees us to consider much more comprehensively all aspects of human nature—not only those that pertain to the sex life, or those that pertain to physical status (organ inferiority), or those that pertain to the spiritual and mystical nature—but the whole of man's nature, including these aspects and others. The particular phenomena that earlier psychoanalytic theories had not sufficiently taken into account and explained were those relating to the individual's relationships with others and his relationship with himself. We focus on the individual in his human environment or social setting in its broad sense. We are convinced that neurosis originates in and remains essentially a disturbance in human relations.

We conceive of personality as acquiring structure in response to environmental conditions. This concept of structure is somewhat analogous to the physicist's concept of atomic structure as consisting of elements and forces tending to maintain the structure and to effect function in relation to other bodies. Each personality has its own unique psychic elements and forces that maintain the integrity of the structure. Each personality functions in accordance with its individual characteristics in relation to other personalities.

We make another important step in viewing human nature. We break with the arbitrary assignment of specific innate psychological differences between men and women on the basis of sex alone. Anthropological and sociological studies have produced convincing evidence that what have been taken for fundamental psychosexual differences are preponderantly the consequence of external cultural influences. Our experience in psychoanalysis shows us that these differences are not rooted in the male and female constitution.

The crucial period in personality development is early childhood; the child is malleable and the human environment is the decisive factor in character formation. A relatively good psychic environment favors development of a strong nucleus of personality which leads to expansion and greater fulfillment. In a poor, barren, or obstructive psychic environment the inner core of personality is unsubstantial and shaky; this leads to the development of a neurotic character structure. The individual who has had quite a good start may encounter overwhelmingly disadvantageous conditions in later childhood or adolescence that he may not have sufficient strength to cope with, and neurotic tendencies may develop. On the other hand, a child in whom weaknesses in structure have begun to develop may come into a life situation so favorable that he is able to develop more strongly. As a rule, however, the early outlines in character formation in an unfavorable environment tend to become set and confirmed.

In the course of time an enormous and complicated elaboration is effected in order to strengthen inner weakness. This serves in later life situations that actually have no relation to the original unfavorable environment. So there comes to be a marked discrepancy between an individual's concept of his present environment and the realities of that environment. Also, in the course of time the individual's potential mental and emotional capacities to deal with life as it really is have increased enormously. But he feels and behaves and acts according to the established patterns of his character structure as it developed under the original unfavorable conditions. Here is another discrepancy, an internal one, between

64

the neurotic personality and the potentially strong and healthy personality.

We keep these discrepancies in view and focus mainly on the difficulties that beset him in his inner life and the consequent difficulties in his relationships with others, rather than on the external environmental situation. For whatever his external situation may be, favorable or unfavorable, he does not see it realistically nor can he realistically mobilize his best resources to cope with it. So while we focus on environmental factors in childhood in attempting to understand what is going on in personality development in the formative stages, we focus on the accomplished fact of the present neurotic structure when it is already developed.

Now let us consider personality development in its early phases. In the very young infant evidences of self seem to be limited to his reactions to physical well-being and physical discomfort. Day by day, week by week, and month by month immature reasoning, thinking, planning, and discrimination come into play. We say the baby is getting to be somebody, a person. He has spontaneous and original impulses that are the expressions of a self in the process of developing. He fumbles, experiments, embarks on various undertakings and adventures, tries himself out in this or that situation, devises projects, seeking always to extend his experience. The more he feels himself to be active and able and effective, the more he wants to experience and the stronger is his urge to grow in his feeling of himself.

65

He notices people around him and begins to know who they are and what they do for him and to him. Then he begins to differentiate between people according to their dealings with him and between different attitudes of the same person toward him. If their ways are benign and understanding and encouraging, he evolves free and natural ways of functioning and a sense of well-being and sureness and confidence in himself.

In view of his factual immaturity and relative weakness, his strongest needs are personal warmth, reliability, and regard for his immaturity. As his judgment and reasoning develop he needs understanding, respect, and justice. These qualities and capacities in those who take care of him mean genuine love for him, which he appreciates and understands. Such would be the ideal psychic environment. However, these perfect conditions rarely exist in our society. Although we have learned scientifically to control conditions for the best development of other living things—plants and animals—we cannot artificially provide perfect conditions for human beings. This is the great hazard in human life.

What are unfavorable psychic conditions in the early environment? The closest and most influential relationship in the child's early life is with his parents or those who take the place of parents, such as relatives, nurses, guardians, institution authorities, etc. The most potent adverse influences are the shortcomings of such persons —their inexperience and inability to give genuine love to the child for himself alone with no ulterior or spurious aims; intense "love" and adoration; unreliability and inconsistency in regard to understanding, guidance, and rational discipline; overindulgence; oversolicitude; favoritism; capriciousness; unpredictability and injustice when the spoiled child runs wild.

Parents sometimes demand intense love and devotion which the child cannot give; he thus fails to live up to exorbitant expectations and is rejected and made to feel wanting or guilty. He lives in a sort of emotional alternating current that goes on and off, in which he can only be confused. Active antagonism is obviously frightening as are humiliations, ridicule, contempt, inappropriate use of authority, and too rigid or cruel discipline. Excessive physical punishment is a real hardship and does affect personality development. However, psychological discipline that cramps, frustrates, and crushes the child's feeling of his value as a human being is far worse. Overemphasis on and excessive expectations in conventional social behavior and school performance give the child a feeling that he is no good as he is, but is worth something only if he comes up to arbitrary standards. Inattention, coldness, and remoteness in parents are likely to set up a feeling of vagueness and eeriness in the child's feeling about himself. He gets no feeling of reality about his existence as a person if he does not see himself as real and important in the eyes of others.

In addition to these adverse psychological conditions, many parental attitudes bear the imprint of general cultural prejudices and distortions of human values common in the community, state, country, or civilization at large. For instance, the following attitudes are frequently communicated through parents: a preference for boys and a prejudice against girls, or vice versa; attaching special values to personal appearance and physical development; intense competitive strivings for popularity, dates, high marks at school, educational accomplishment; the possession of money, fashionable clothes, material things that are the criteria of "belonging"; pernicious political ideologies; dishonesty, cynicism, decadence, which may taint a whole culture or civilization.

These attitudes and prejudices are not always mediated by parents, but may be encountered outside the home. They are likely to affect the child's sense of his own worth if emotional factors in the home have already contributed to an inner sense of precariousness. But if relationships in the home have contributed to the development of a strong and secure inner core of personality, the child may not be much affected by adverse conditions from cultural sources outside. Other adverse influences of the same nature as those exercised by parents are projected by siblings, other relatives, and servants in close contact with the child.

Normally, children are aware of being small and less capable than those who are older and taller and able to accomplish more than children do. Nevertheless, under favorable environmental conditions, they have an inner sense of personal importance and value. They cope with life with originality, freedom, and strong persistence to learn and overcome obstacles. If the environment does not present positive threats, the child's feeling of disadvantage usually disappears in the course of later development and successful accomplishment as his experience broadens in school and social life.

According to the extent to which the relationships of others toward the child fall short of being favorable, feelings of insecurity arise in him. According to the extent to which conditions are positively against the interests of the child's development, his inner feeling is one of real peril or of fear for his survival as a person. Such feelings of insecurity, peril or fear give rise to inferiority feelings. This expression is used rather commonly to refer to simple feelings of being at a disadvantage or feelings of inadequacy but it has much stronger implications. Inferiority feelings involve feelings of being of little or no worth as a human being, of not having the status that others have, of being despised and cast out of a place with others.

Since there is no such thing as perfect understanding or pure essence of love for a child, inferiority feelings are probably very common in childhood. Those that persist have their origin in a sense of real danger to the self. The child feels helpless, abandoned, alone, isolated; he feels there is no one to go to who can be trusted and the whole world is hostile to him. He inevitably develops a sense of hostility to the world. The state of feeling helpless, isolated, and hostile is called *basic anxiety*. Basic anxiety is the motivating force that starts the neurotic process going. In order to allay basic anxiety, the child mobilizes his resources and energies, and his attitudes and behavior toward others are modified in the interest of insuring his safety.

69

There is a deep human need to orient oneself in relation to other human beings. We are beginning to discern phenomena in human relationships that express this need and that are manifested in three kinds of movement in relation to others: (1) tendencies to move toward others in affection, trust, and interdependency; (2) tendencies to move against others in opposition to them and to stand up for one's own interests, and defeat others; (3) tendencies to move away from others in order to cultivate oneself as a separate entity. These three types of movement were first identified in exaggerated manifestations in disturbed, anxiety-ridden individuals. They appeared as compulsive and indiscriminate. If the individual was frustrated in expression and satisfaction of them, he felt intense discomfort.

Without the element of exaggeration, the tendency to go toward others is expressed in being friendly and considerate, in being in close, affectionate rapport, in trusting people, asking for help when it is needed, giving help, in yielding to others when it is appropriate. The tendency to go against others is expressed in standing up to others, insisting on one's own rights, pushing one's own claims, competing with others with the aim of excelling, protesting and fighting if necessary when one is ill-used, being alert and on guard against insidious attack. The tendency to move away from others is expressed in withdrawing and maintaining personal privacy. It satisfies natural interests in self-sufficiency and independence, natural needs for solitude, respite from the impact of the outer world, contemplation necessary for maintaining contact with oneself and for developing one's own creative capacities.

A child who has a sense of inner precariousness or basic anxiety has to regulate his movements in human relationships according to his need for safety, and his movements in relationships with others become invested with forces and energies necessary to attain it. When he moves toward others, he is driven by intense needs for affection, needs to find someone to cling to in undue dependence, to be excessively compliant, appeasing, placating, and conciliatory. When he moves against others, he feels he must dominate, override, get the best of others, and fight for supremacy. Movement away from others is expressed in extreme withdrawal, pulling away, covering up, and hiding. These are called *neurotic trends*. They are neurotic because, provoked by an inner state of trepidation and alarm, they are imbued with excessive tensions and are carried out with an excessive amount of energy in striving for the particular goal of each trend, which in each case means safety. A literal paraphrase of the term *neurotic* would be "full of nervousness," or "full of nervous tension."

Neurotic trends are characterized by constant and intense preoccupation with the goal of the trend and with the means to achieve it, and they are pursued with relentless tenacity. This is the quality of compulsiveness. They also have the quality of indiscriminateness, that is, the individual must get everyone to like him, or he must be defiant and aggressive on all occasions, or he must protect himself by withdrawing as a blanket policy. And

71

finally, when the individual is frustrated in his neurotic aims and activities, he feels unsafe, anxious, or panicky. He may not feel anxiety as such but it may be transmuted into a depression, or an outburst of rage, or a state of paralyzing blankness, or disorders of bodily function.

Because of basic anxiety all three aspects of movement in relation to others become compulsive and indiscriminate. In individual children, some one group of trends with their special needs and aims is emphasized and adopted as a preferred way to cope with the environment. Whether constitutional variations in individual children play a role in the selection of a particular group of trends is not clear at present; this question will have to wait upon further research. Whatever may come to light, it is fairly certain that the influence of environment is the prime factor in necessitating the adoption of some means to insure safety. So we see different types of solution of the problem of anxiety in childhood—in the approval-seeking, obedient, submissive child; the rebellious, defiant child; and the quiet, withdrawn child. Later developments show that no matter which general type of reaction first emerges, neurotic trends of the other two categories have also developed although they may not be in evidence.

There is a great expansion of needs in the course of time. All people with whom the neurotic individual comes in contact take on the aspect of "prospects" for the satisfaction of neurotic needs, and all situations represent mainly a potential field in which to operate on these terms. If the individual is predominantly approval-seeking and compliant, he must get everyone to like him, whether or not others have likable and valuable qualities, whether or not the individual really likes them, and whether or not they are of real importance to him. He must always be approved of; he must always be indulged and protected and privileged. Neurotic aggressiveness drives a person to offensive attitudes and behavior toward everybody, whether or not they are threatening and antagonistic to him, and whether or not there is anything necessary and constructive to be gained in defeating others. Trends to isolate oneself from others dictate extreme independence; even when the individual is really in need of human contact, he must guard his privacy to the point of foregoing necessary help. The same general principle holds true regardless of the relative importance of situations. The neurotic person will behave in the same compulsive way whether he is making a trivial purchase or pursuing his lifework.

Each trend is implemented, in time, with special strategies, tactics and maneuvers appropriate to it. These are seen more clearly in individuals in whom trends of one category predominate, and in whom trends of other categories are kept out of sight or repressed. The predominantly compliant individual develops, in the course of time and experience, endearing, flattering and cajoling methods; he goes to great lengths to be submissive, self-effacing, never to put forward any claims for himself. The predominantly aggressive individual develops special alertness to the weaknesses, flaws, and sensitivities of others in order to increase his

73

advantage; he cultivates the arts and skills of the fighter, and callously overrides the rights and interests of others. Inattention, coldness, great guardedness in respect to approaches of others, extreme independence and self-sufficiency are methods employed by the predominantly detached individual to keep a distance between himself and others.

Associated with each neurotic trend are special sensitivities, fears, and inhibitions. People with strong compliancy trends are especially sensitive to displeasure or anger in others, are fearful of anything approaching an argument or fight, and are unable to be demanding or aggressive. Those who are mainly compulsively aggressive are wary of affectionate, considerate behavior and treatment and are generally inhibited in any expression of softer feelings. People who are predominantly detached are extremely uncomfortable when it is necessary to be in close contact with others; they dread anything which threatens their independence and self-sufficiency, and they are quite strictly limited in respect to any kind of real personal intimacy.

The neurotic individual evolves special falsely rationalized values for neurotic trends in order to justify them and in order not to see them in their true light. For if he did, he would have to realize that they are indefensible. He comes to regard them as sensible, logical, necessary, unavoidable, attractive, praiseworthy, and superior to other ways. And conversely, he regards natural healthy ways as inferior, impractical, senseless or positively immoral.

74

With the development of neurotic trends as safety devices, basic anxiety is apt to recede into the background of consciousness, although in some individuals it is felt as a secret, lurking sense of being a lonely, friendless child in a hostile world. In others, it is completely lost sight of but persists as a smoldering core in the personality. In the course of time it acquires accruals of intensity arising from various sources. The very persistence of the means to insure safety keeps alive and enhances the illusion of loneliness and danger and the constant practice of neurotic maneuvers reinforces the sense of driving necessity to protect oneself. The success of the devices comes to have the significance of proof of their validity. "It always works, so it must be right." Undiscerning and uncritical friends subscribe to the compulsive needs of the neurotic individual and unwittingly support him in his notion of necessity and validity.

In the pursuance of neurotic aims and the practice of neurotic ways, the individual has not developed natural, appropriate ways of dealing with life. Hence, when his neurotic devices fail him he has nothing else and is really helpless. He is then exposed to his worst terror—being completely at the mercy of the world. Ernie Pyle writes of the reaction to the sound of a shell when soldiers are under fire: "The sound produces a kind of horror that is something more than mere fright. It is a confused form of acute desperation." Just as the soldier is helpless in this situation, so the neurotic is essentially helpless—because he actually has no means to fend off the hostility of the world.

75

The neurotic individual's expectations of danger from the outside are enhanced because his impulses are supercharged. He would surrender completely and abjectly in the interests of dependency; his aggressive drives would lead him to antagonize and alienate others; his tendencies to isolate himself would set him off further and further in loneliness. So his very safety devices, while warding off dangers, constitute at the same time a threat to safety. Compliancy trends lead to being exploited; aggressiveness stirs up counterattack and alienates affectionate people; and detachment tendencies lead to ostracism. But the neurotic individual does not realize that what happens to him is to a large extent the result of his own behavior and activities; nevertheless, he suffers from these consequences.

In addition, the simultaneous existence in the individual of neurotic trends belonging to these three categories leads to the generation of more anxiety from internal sources. He has three means of achieving safety all of which are at variance with each other. Getting approval and establishing clinging, dependent relationships constitute attempts to achieve safety by means that are diametrically opposite to rebellious, offensive, and aggressive tactics. And these means which bring him into close contact with others, one in excessive friendliness, the other in enmity, are at variance in turn with his compulsive needs to withdraw and isolate himself. Isolation endangers compliant attitudes as well as aggressive drives because it interferes with the individual's attempts at getting affection and protection on the one hand, and prevents him from maintaining his aggressive position on the other.

If impulses from discrepant and incompatible sources arise simultaneously, they can create a most serious dilemma, the dilemma of *conflict*. The individual has no choice of compulsive means to insure safety since the forces involved in all his compulsive ways are equally strong. When drives aiming at different goals are felt in full force, the individual has the experience of being torn apart, of going to pieces. Conflict felt less acutely precipitates confusion and anxiety. The individual feels threatened with the breakdown of his defense system and the penalty for such a breakdown is total vulnerability in a hostile world.

The neurotic individual must avoid such a calamity at all costs. The rest of this discussion of the neurotic character structure deals with the individual's attempts to avoid awareness of conflict, of the contradictory qualities, needs, aims, and values of his incompatible neurotic trends. He must create the illusion of integrity, harmony, or unity in order to maintain his equilibrium and avoid the threat of disintegration.

We call the means he employs to accomplish this his *attempts at solution of conflict*. When we speak of the neurotic solutions of conflict, we mean false or pseudo solutions, for there is no real solution of conflict except the undoing of the tangled web of irreconcilable neurotic trends. We identify four main ways in which the neurotic individual attempts to solve inner conflict: (1) predominance of one set of major neurotic trends; (2) ex-

77

ternalization of internal problems; (3) construction of an idealized image of the self; (4) detachment from emotional relationships with others.

In the first instance, the predominance of one set of major neurotic trends, the individual admits neurotic trends of one general category into consciousness, though without a true appreciation of their significance, and represses contradictory trends. He can thus think of himself as one kind of person and establish a feeling of unity, of not being divided. On the surface such people seem to present definite, consistent types of personality —the affectionate, compliant type, the aggressive type, or the detached type. In such "typing" we must remember that the obvious traits are only the predominating ones, and that incompatible trends exist as tremendously potent underground forces which make themselves felt in the inner life, though completely unrecognized by the individual and vehemently denied as quite alien to him.

Inhibitions are the chief clues to repressed trends. The person in whom compliance and dependency predominate will be unable to stand up for himself and fight; the aggressive type of person is unable to yield and seek the good graces of others. Both types are frequently unable to contain themselves in solitude. The withdrawn type of person is unable to establish intimate personal relationships with others either for approval or in aggressive action. Repressed trends are bound to precipitate tensions and to find expression in some form or other. Slips of the tongue, inadvertent remarks, forgetting and

78

absent-mindedness reveal unknown and unacknowledged tendencies. Phantasies and dreams contain material that helps us to identify and understand repressed neurotic tendencies. The rationalized values for the predominating trends are greatly reinforced, and the repressed trends are devaluated to the point of abhorrence.

Externalization of inner problems means that the individual manages to remain unaware of his neurotic trends and conflicts by focusing on other people's difficulties, their troubles, their weaknesses. He usually feels that his environment is in a turmoil, that the world is out of joint. He may take a morbid satisfaction in such matters. He tends to interfere, criticize, advise, instruct, apparently helpfully. But there is always a quality of indiscriminateness, indiscretion, and tactlessness that is the clue to a driven need to avoid awareness of difficulties within himself. He tends to put the blame for whatever he suffers in consequence of his own inner conflicts upon external conditions, and he may feel helpless and swamped by them. He feels he is tired and nervous because of his job situation, because of the impossible disposition of his boss, his friend, or his wife. He would say that city life is too hectic, that country life is too dull. He believes he would get on better socially and in his work if only he had better clothes or the right connections or if only his wife was more helpful. He is convinced that he flies into an ungovernable temper only because someone provoked him, that he married only because his wife inveigled him into it.

He looks to the outside for the solution to his difficulties—a change of location, a different wife, a devoted friend who would understand him—and he busies himself manipulating and changing the external circumstances of his life. Frequently women believe that having a baby would dispel discontent and boredom under the impression that, if they had someone to live for, their difficulties would disappear. Whatever is really disadvantageous in the external situation is never tackled realistically; constructive changes are not undertaken and, above all, the individual never looks into himself to figure out his responsibility, to discover how he himself could bring about constructive changes.

The person who attempts to solve conflicts by way of creating an idealized image of himself rises above his inner difficulties by sustaining himself in phantasies of being a superpersonality. He gathers his material for this construction of his personality from the falsely rationalized values he has created for his neurotic traits. The idealized image is a merger of discrepant characteristics which he does not recognize as discrepant but conceives of only as virtues which he arrogates to himself.

For instance, a woman saw herself as a "benevolent business woman with a broad social outlook." Analysis of her personality revealed intense needs for approval and compulsive tendencies to comply and submit to others. She was overconsiderate and self-sacrificing, exaggeratedly helpful and overindulgent toward others. This was her "benevolence." She also had strong hostile

80

aggressive tendencies, expressed mainly in hard-boiled, exploitive business practices of which she was quite proud, and in subtlely sadistic attitudes and behavior in social life and intimate relationships. This was the "business woman." She also tended to stand aloof from others, to take the position of a bystander and onlooker in human affairs, to be unduly independent. These characteristics were some manifestation of her withdrawal tendencies. She had taken traits from each main neurotic trend, converted them into virtues—in her own estimation—and thus characterized herself to her own satisfaction in the thumbnail sketch of a "benevolent business woman with a broad social outlook." In addition, her attention was almost exclusively directed to problems outside of herself. Her first statement upon undertaking analysis was that she felt she was entirely well adjusted, that she had no personal difficulties but would like to see if analysis would solve two problems, one in her business life and the other connected with her domestic situation.

The fourth main way in which the neurotic individual attempts to eliminate conflict is to avoid all emotional involvement with others. This constitutes an attempt to ignore or deny contradictory trends by seeing to it that no occasion arises in which emotions would come into play. It is similar to the basic neurotic trend—to withdraw from a threatening environment as a safety device—but is practiced to avoid the danger of becoming aware of inner feelings. Avoiding all emotional involvement, the individual permits himself only limited dealings with

81

others through certain limited avenues of approach. These are suggested by pressure needs of other drives which must also be satisfied.

For instance, if there are very strong needs for affection, the individual may adopt sexuality as the basis of relationships with others. In this he maintains emotional detachment, satisfies needs for closeness to others, and has the illusion that he is participating in a love relationship. Or the individual may limit himself to intellectual interests with others, or business dealings, or other practical affairs as common ground and make them the whole point of contact. Those who are involved in such relationships with him always have the impression that they do not really know how he feels about anything— they do not know him as a whole person.

The neurotic solution of conflict is a process that takes time to evolve. We see individuals who have not yet come to a solution, or who show some evidence that they are beginning to hit upon one, or who flit from one solution to another experimentally. All four solutions are usually utilized to some extent by the same person, sometimes with emphasis on one type of solution.

Although neurotic solutions of conflict are devised for the purpose of holding the personality together and maintaining equilibrium, they in their turn constitute defenses that must be maintained, else the individual feels endangered or upset. A variety of secondary defenses function as additional insurance against becoming aware of conflict. These are the cultivation of blind spots by which the individual can remain blissfully unaware of contradictions and discrepancies; rationalization, by which he explains away inconsistencies by plausible but spurious justifications.

He also compartmentalizes his thinking, that is, he sees no inconsistency in behaving and acting one way in private, another way in public; one way toward members of the family, another way toward friends and acquaintances outside the family; one way toward social equals, another way toward those he does not consider his social equals, etc. Another common defense is to claim arbitrary and unquestioned rightness for everything he feels and does, including all his flagrant contradictions and inconsistencies. He may attempt to protect himself from awareness of uncontrollable impulses by maintaining an iron control over his feelings.

Still another way of avoiding recognition of contradictions is to reduce everything to total inconsequentiality by being cynical or flippant. The individual tends to take the position that there is no right or wrong, no truth or falsehood, that nothing matters enough to constitute an issue. Finally he may avoid issues concerning his inner problems by resorting to extreme elusiveness. People who exhibit this tendency are slippery, devious, so highly circumstantial that their part in events is lost in a mass of detail.

These elaborations in the development of the neurotic character structure have many consequences—some of them completely unrecognized by the individual himself because he cannot face the issues of cause and effect. Some of these consequences are partially felt and dimly appreciated as having some connection with anxiety. Others are felt acutely and distressingly. These last constitute the specific, outspoken complaints and symptoms of neurosis. I shall discuss these consequences all together, and you will see which ones the neurotic individual would be blind to, and why, and which ones he would complain of. The ones he complains of are, in effect, the price he pays for the ones he needs to retain unrecognized as essential to the integrity of the neurotic structure.

In general, the development and the upkeep of neurotic patterns consume a prodigious amount of energy which could otherwise be used in the development of real capacities and gifts, in the cultivation of good human relationships, and in the enjoyment of life. This wasteful expenditure of energy brings about a sense of futility, a feeling that one is not getting enough out of life or a vague, sometimes acute discontent. There are also likely to be pervasive feelings of strain and fatigue, and a need for more rest and more sleep than is required by the average healthy person.

The powerful crosscurrents underlying unresolved conflicts result in inertia, ineffectualness, and indecision. The individual is unable to settle on a course in life and exert his best efforts in some definite, undeviating direction. Spontaneous initiative and sustained action are extremely difficult. If initiative is not paralyzed, it is short-lived and shifting. The individual tends to avoid constructive effort. It takes so much out of him since he has to reckon with the exhausting intensity with which

84

he applies himself and with the counterpull of opposing impulses. He is apt to feel jammed, or as if caught in a vise. People sometimes complain of a feeling that they are stagnating or unable to get on in their work or profession.

Moral values are blunted because the individual becomes habituated to false justifications, rationalizations, pretenses, and spurious defenses. Because he manipulates his values according to the exigencies of neurotic needs, he is apt to become cynical and to lose faith or belief in everything, including himself. Since he is generally motivated by the necessity to avoid anxiety, conscious and unconscious exploitation of others is inevitable. Truth and honesty with others and with himself go by the board.

Neurotic persons are necessarily highly egocentric because their needs come first. This is so even if needs to be self-sacrificing are conspicuous, for the unduly self-sacrificing person frustrates others from participating on equal terms and inhibits them in developing their own resources. This egocentricity is exaggerated to enormous arrogance in the process of false solution of conflicts. In general, avoidance of awareness of inner problems requires explicitly that the individual see nothing wrong with himself. Each type of solution has its particular form of arrogance. Baffling guilt feelings, which are quite common, often spring from unconscious crookedness, although frequently the reasons for guilt feelings are assigned to some circumstance in which the individual is factually innocent.

At the core of every neurotic personality there is more or less hopelessness. This stems from being caught in conflicts that cannot really be resolved in view of the individual's deep feelings of helplessness, isolation, and hostility. Besides, his rigid patterns in human relations and in whatever he undertakes always bring about the same frustration, so he is likely to feel doomed to frustration. Neurotic development takes him further and further away from himself, so that he becomes shadowy and unreal to himself. He has no real hold on the direction of his life and no notion of what he really wants, for he is in the grip of forces driving him toward the goal of safety only.

Despair may be so abysmal that he may succumb to complete resignation, settle down quietly, and even feel somewhat at peace. He "accepts" his fate but forfeits the fullness of his real capacities and the real richness of his nature. But hopelessness, despair, and resignation may lead to bitterness and rage against fate, which may be focused on those who are participating in life and enjoying it. In an attempt to reclaim or salvage some feeling of self, the individual turns destructive and sadistic in revenge. Sadistic tendencies are directed not only toward others in overt or subtle ways but also toward the self.

As further consequences of unresolved conflicts there are many fears, some of them diffuse, some of them specific and sharply focused. The individual feels vaguely fearful whenever a safety device is threatened, when a compromise solution is in danger of failing him, or when defenses are jeopardized. He fears the loss of neurotic satisfactions, as for instance in any disturbance of his idealized image and the gratifications he gets from it in his imagination. He fears exposure of his false claims, for to him this would mean certain ridicule and humiliation in the eyes of others and in his own eyes. Since his equilibrium is usually shaky and requires constant support and stabilization, he is always afraid of being upset.

Some specific and sharply focused fears connected with certain external situations and circumstances arise from inner fears which are externalized and symbolized. The dread of being in high places and of falling is usually connected with fear of loss of equilibrium, of falling from the pinnacle of perfection one has arrogated to oneself, fear of collapse of one's illusions, of falling into the abyss of self-degradation. Fears of being in open places may be connected with fears of being alone, being separated from others and deserted. Fears of being in confined places may be connected with the fears of being hemmed in, constricted, being deprived of space which are felt by markedly detached people.

These fears do not usually have one simple direct derivation, but may be compounded of fears arising from several sources. Fears of germs, infection, or dirt in any form are similarly traced to inner sensitivities, fears, and inhibitions. Seemingly intractable, externalized fears are likely to have compound derivations in the neurotic structure. These fears force the individual to extreme precautions which are expressed in avoiding contact with certain things, in compulsive hand washing or bathing and sometimes quite bizarre means to avoid contamination. The thousand-and-one superstitions concerning good luck or bad luck cause some people to adopt peculiar ritualistic mannerisms and behavior. These become conspicuous and sometimes intolerably burdensome and annoying.

Generally speaking, the sense of being helplessly caught in conflicts and the resultant feeling of impotent rage are the components of depressions. Rage may be quite deeply repressed; the depression is then diffuse and unfocused and the individual is lost in feelings of abysmal self-pity. When rage and despair are more conscious and destructive impulses are more openly in play, depressions may bring the individual to ruminations on suicide or to an actual attempt at self-destruction.

Other outspoken neurotic manifestations are general inhibitions such as inability to think, to concentrate, to make decisions, to embark on fresh enterprises, to learn something new. Specific inhibitions are related to specific fears or phobias, such as inability to go to the upper floors of high buildings, to ride on elevators and subway trains, to walk in the open street, to be alone. Inability to go to sleep has a particular meaning for different people. A common one is the driving necessity to anticipate the next day's activities and plan them to the last detail so that the individual will be prepared for everything with a foolproof schedule. Or, a young man may stay awake the whole night through in order to keep an eye on the world while others sleep. He drops off to sleep when he hears the milkman come up the street, with the feeling that the milkman is awake and he, the "watchman," can now give over.

Frequently symptoms are directly connected with relationships with others, such as inability to get along, feeling always an outsider who is excluded by others, intense shyness, uncontrollable aggressiveness; terrible, frightening impulses to harm others, undue dependence on others, inability to love, inability to hate. In this category are specific disturbances in sex life such as frigidity and painful intercourse in women, impotence and premature ejaculations in men, compulsive sexual promiscuity, aversion to sex relationships with the opposite sex and a preference for relationships with persons of one's own sex, and undifferentiated sexuality, sometimes called bisexuality.

Many physical manifestations are the expression of tensions precipitated by repressed anxiety or rage such as flushing or pallor, sweating, palpitation, high blood pressure, low blood pressure, muscular tensions of all sorts, severe cramping pains, especially around the neck and shoulders and lower back, lump in throat, shortness of breath, sinking feelings, fainting, sleeping attacks, gastrointestinal upsets, constipation, diarrhea, nausea, headache, migraine attacks, and some functional disorders of the reproductive organs. Among the latter are painful and irregular menstruation, scanty or suppressed menses or profuse and too frequent menses, painful erection in men, prostatic turgidity, and some cases of prostatitis.

Some neurotic manifestations represent a subsidiary

89

solution the individual has hit upon, some comforting and narcotizing agent he has found useful in allaying anxiety but which has come to be uncontrollable and harmful. In this category alcoholism and drug addiction are outstanding symptoms. There are also some less obvious activities that help one to forget one's worries such as engaging hectically and compulsively in social activities, hobbies, or work. The clue to the compulsive nature of these activities lies in the fact that the individual tends to plunge into the activity with exhausting "enthusiasm." He does not really enjoy it for what it is and thus cannot feel a sense of recreation, and as a result the experience leaves him with a feeling of "ashes in the mouth."

You will have noticed that I have used few of the familiar diagnostic terms in this chapter such as psychoneurosis, neurasthenia, obsessive-compulsive states, claustrophobia, agoraphobia. These terms in themselves describe the manifestation in Greek derivatives or other language compounds; but thinking in terms of symptoms does not offer any real guide to understanding and treatment. Our interest lies in attempting to understand the character structure as a whole, its development, and the dynamics of the neurotic process in their present form and complexity. By this route we get light on the meaning of the particular manifestation in the individual character structure.

Finally, there is the neurotic individual who has no obvious disturbances of the kind mentioned. You will ask, "Is he neurotic?" Yes, he is a "successful" neurotic.

Such a person shows very obvious contradictions in his character and gross deviations in human relationships. But he has been successful in blinding himself to them, successful in operating with his false solutions of conflict, and successful in making himself practically immune to disturbance from the outside and from within. Many such people live calm lives; they may do valuable work, and they do not experience anything out of the way in their scheme of life. They would say they haven't a nerve in their body. Nevertheless, there is always a discrepancy between the life they lead, their actual achievements, and the kind of relationships they have and the fuller, richer, deeper life possible for them by a greater satisfaction in their achievements, and better relationships with others.

The deficits in character and achievement and relationships are the outstanding factors in the "successful" neurotic. Basic anxiety exists deeply buried and unexperienced. It could be felt in some crisis or some unforeseen turn of events or even in some trivial contretemps. When this happens, it comes as a stunning surprise and is quite incomprehensible.

An example of this is that of a man who came to analysis at the behest of a close associate who was genuinely appreciative of him and was concerned about some of his peculiarities. The patient felt he was completely "well adjusted" but he had had one upsetting experience, five years previously. He had been lecturing to students. A boy in the class asked an irrelevant question. The teacher's mind suddenly went blank, and he was overwhelmed by total panic. He turned blindly to the blackboard and made some illegible scrawls for a few moments and then the bell rang for the end of the session. After dismissing the class, he went home, and was in bed for two weeks with intractable diarrhea. He recovered completely from this physical upset and returned to work.

In this chapter I have presented a somewhat detailed elaboration of our present theory of neurosis. The main outline in neurotic structure and the forces involved have been stressed. The discussion suffers somewhat from condensation. It may give an impression of simplicity to some or of great complexity to others. The latter comes nearer to the truth. Our experience in attempting to help the patient to extricate himself from his neurosis convinces us that his entanglements are tremendously complex. We believe that our formulations, which are based on dynamic principles originally discovered by Freud, include and explain many phenomena in the neurotic system hitherto ignored or not satisfactorily accounted for. While the essentials in our formulations can be presented more or less briefly, the manifold details of neurotic involvement need much further investigation. These are the directions in which we continue to work.

What Are Your Doubts About Analysis?

HAROLD KELMAN, M.D.

MANY people who think of undertaking an analysis hesitate because of certain doubts, fears, and misgivings. From questions asked after lectures on psychoanalysis and by patients in consultations we find that the following matters are the most frequent cause of concern: the expense in money and time; the effectiveness of analytic treatment; the harmful effects that analysis might produce. In this chapter we shall take up these questions in the order of frequency with which they usually occur.

The matter of finances is often the first practical consideration. You may doubt that you can afford an analysis. It is true that many people, even with careful budgeting, are still excluded from receiving analytic help for financial reasons. There are a number of causes for this unfortunate situation, long a matter of serious concern

93

to analysts. Assuming, however, that you do have the means for an analysis but still feel that the fee is too much, you might think about it as you do about other forms of medical therapy. The total cost of an acute or chronic illness may be greater than that of an analysis but you do not ask, "Is it necessary?" or "Should I spend the money?" Because a physical illness is so real and tangible and the discomfort so obvious and acute, it is regarded as quite natural to do something about it at once. Further, you feel justified in your decision because the doctor does something obvious and immediate for you. He may give you medicine, put you to bed, or operate on you; in any case, you feel that you can legitimately expect concrete results in a reasonable time. You also take as a matter of course the doctor's bills and the attendant expenditures for medications, hospitalization, and operations.

With analysis the situation is quite different. You may have definite complaints such as a fear of high places, attacks of anxiousness, or headaches, but even though these symptoms are quite real to you, no one else can see them. A checkup with your doctor may reveal nothing wrong with you of a physical nature. Because you have not been taught to think in terms of psychic illness you may conclude that your complaints are purely imaginary or, at any rate, not very serious and certainly not of the type to warrant the expense or possibly the financial sacrifices that analytic therapy would entail. You may be confirmed in this attitude by your friends and relatives. For all these reasons you

94

may think of analysis in terms of cost rather than of benefits to be derived.

When you add up the total cost of an analysis, it may seem like a very large sum. However, if you will keep in mind that you will be paying for it in small sums, weekly or monthly, spread out over a period of time, the amount will not loom so large. Thinking in these terms and with careful budgeting, you may find that an analysis is within your means.

Sometimes when people feel that they cannot afford an analysis, closer investigation reveals that their judgment is dictated by irrational, unconscious fears. Such persons may be motivated by an unconscious fear of becoming destitute, which makes them adverse to parting with anything. Irrational feelings of incompetence to regain what they might spend make it a stringent necessity to hold on to what they have. Or they may regard themselves as so unworthy that they do not feel entitled to spend a large amount or even any amount of money on themselves.

In many cases analysis has proved to be a good investment and has paid dividends. Not uncommonly there is an increase in efficiency and productivity with resultant favorable changes in the patient's job situation. His earnings increase and his ability to handle his funds improves. Irrational spending or saving stops: he uses his money wisely. In cases where money was spent on physical illnesses that were an expression of underlying emotional problems, or where financial loss was incurred through absence from work, these expenses stop. However, such results, though tangible, should not be considered as primary. Increased happiness and lessened misery are objectives whose value cannot be calculated in figures.

After you have decided what you can pay, you will naturally discuss it with the analyst. In deciding on his fee, he will take into consideration whether you have correctly evaluated your ability to pay for treatment. If he feels that your evaluation is not realistic and that you really do not have the means to pay for an analysis or, on the other hand, that you can afford a higher fee than the one you suggested, he will tell you so. On the basis of such a discussion, you will arrive at an agreement as to what you both consider a legitimate fee.

Some people are doubtful about undertaking analysis because they feel it takes up too much time. Limitations of time may be a real impediment to your being able to avail yourself of analytic help. Your working hours may be so long that you simply have no spare time. Your schedule may make it difficult to find an analyst who is free when you are. Analysts are cognizant of this problem and try to reserve early morning, lunch, and evening hours for persons with tight schedules. They ask other patients whose arrangements are more flexible to give preference to those who are bound by rigid time schedules.

However, a number of people think they do not have enough time for an analysis. Careful examination of your schedule may reveal that you have more time than you thought or that by budgeting what time you do have you may be able to carry an analytic program. You may discover that you allow time to slip through your fingers, take much too long to do certain things, or occupy yourself with a lot of unnecessary activities. A little self-discipline may be all that is necessary to make available the time for analytic treatment. Scrutiny of your time schedule may lead to the recognition that the way time is used, or rather misused, just doesn't make sense. Awareness of this fact may lead to a more thorough self-examination and the desire for analytic assistance. In analysis we frequently see irrational attitudes about time.

You may feel that you are short on time merely at present and have the definite intention to start your analysis at a later date. You may actually be pressed for time, for a longer or shorter period, owing to external circumstances such as illness in the family or because of a genuine desire to first complete a project or to embark on one you already had in mind. But when you go from project to project and there always seem to be external situations that must be taken care of first, then you should try to determine whether your reasons for being so constantly occupied, or more probably preoccupied, are really valid. This is particularly important if your schedule is flexible and, to an objective observer, you seem to have plenty of time.

In very few cases has the time factor proved insurmountable. We can cite many instances in which it was felt at first that analysis was not possible or was at best extremely difficult because of time limitations; yet these patients managed to work out arrangements and carry on their analytic work successfully. Besides, we all know that the busiest people always manage to find time for activities that they really want to pursue.

You may ask: "Doesn't an analysis go on and on and on?" The length of an individual analysis cannot, as a rule, be accurately predicted. It is hard to estimate at the outset the three essential factors upon which its progress and duration depend: the severity of the neurosis, the active participation of the patient, and the analyst's experience with the particular problems that become evident in the course of the analysis. The severity of the neurosis is often difficult to estimate because appearances are deceptive. Even an experienced analyst may err because initially there is much information lacking which, were it available, would change his estimate. An analyst may have a more optimistic outlook than is warranted because at the beginning of the work his patient is eager and willing both during and between analytic sessions. Or the patient may be quick in grasping insights and in seeing them for himself. But all of this often changes when difficult problems arise; then a marked slowing of pace occurs.

On the whole, the average time for an analysis of a severe neurosis is about three years, that is, for the thorough working through of the involved character difficulties presented. This is reckoned from the time analysis is started to its termination. Included in this period are interruptions for vacations, illness, or other circumstances. However, the statistical average of three years may be of limited value to you in gauging the duration of your own analysis. Your neurosis may be more severe than you believed, or it may be less severe. This also holds true for situations where the patient seeks help for some particular problem. In some instances the patient can be given sufficient help in relatively few interviews to enable him to keep on functioning quite well; in others it may be discovered that the problem he presents has so many ramifications that only a thorough analysis will solve it. Also, he may come with only one problem and find after a few interviews that there are a number of others he wants to work through. Under these circumstances treatment would naturally take much longer than was originally estimated.

If you feel that three years constitute an overwhelmingly long period, remember that only a small part of your day will be devoted to analytic work. For the rest, you will be carrying on your usual activities. In time you will come to take the daily or tri-weekly hour in your stride, as well as the months and the years. The more clearly you come to recognize the necessity for your analysis, the meaning it gives to your life, and the results you obtain from it, the less concerned you will be about its duration. Three years does not seem like an inordinate period to invest in your future happiness, nor a particularly long time for the solution of troubles that have been accumulating for thirty or forty years.

Generally it is easier for people to think of a long-term project if it has an educational purpose. It may help you to think of your analysis as part of an educational program with one course. You are the text and the source material. The purpose of the project is to teach you to see yourself as you are, to remove those obstacles in yourself that prevent you from developing your best potentialities.

Distance from centers where analytical help is available is another practical consideration that may make you doubtful about undertaking analysis. Distance alone may not prevent you from receiving some analytic help, but when the problem of time or money or both is added, even limited analytic help is made almost impossible.

With enough time and money you may come at intervals for short periods of concentrated analytic work; you may even move to the city where your analyst resides and remain there until the analysis is terminated. Special arrangements may be made for intensive work at intervals. When the distance is not too great, a patient can be seen for single or double sessions. He can meet with his analyst the night of his arrival and again the next morning and the evening before his departure. In this way he is absent from his job, business, or family for only one day. The results of such work have often proved satisfactory, even though this procedure may have prolonged the duration of the analyses.

Because of the expense involved, the duration of analysis, and the factor of distance, you may be concerned about possible interruption of your analytic work by reason of external circumstances. For instance, you may only have enough money to carry you for two weeks or two months at a time; it may be impossible for you to remain absent from your job or your family any longer than that. There may be interruptions owing to acute illness or, for reasons of health or business, you may have to move too far away to be able to continue work with your analyst. Unexpected drains on your funds may force you to discontinue your analytic work. A job situation or a deadline on a special project might make it impossible for you to devote the necessary time to analysis.

The effect that an interruption of your analysis will have on you depends on a number of factors: the length of the interruption, whether or not you had planned for it, the progress you have already made in your analytic work, and the spirit in which you undertook and continued with it. If you knew that you could work for a short time only, the interruption would be something planned for and expected. You might have preferred to continue, but you would not be concerned or upset if your over-all plan called for short periods of analysis at intervals over a longer period of time. If the spirit in which you sought help was one of real determination combined with the feeling that no matter how long the intervals might be, you would keep returning, you would not be irrationally upset. Nor would limited interruptions, resulting from financial or other external situations already expected, cause much hardship.

If you are well along in your analytic work, an expected temporary or even prolonged interruption will not be unduly disturbing. Solid work done can be a

101

source of satisfaction and form a point from which to continue on your own. You will have an opportunity to get a perspective on yourself, digest what you have learned, develop on the basis of this increased self-knowledge, and continue working at your problems with the analytic equipment you have acquired. This holds true for short or longer interruptions at almost any point in your analysis. Interruptions, then, can have a beneficial effect in many instances. Their disadvantage, of course, lies in prolongation of the work.

Even unexpected interruptions may not be too disturbing if they occur after progress has been made. You may feel at loose ends for a time as you would following a break in any intimate relationship. You may acutely miss the help you have been getting. But in time you will find that you can go along on your own much better than you ever did before. If unexpected interruptions should occur at a period when you are upset by the awareness and the working through of major conflicts, you may have quite a difficult time of it. However, these breaks rarely happen so suddenly that the analyst cannot carry out some helpful preparatory work. In the isolated instances where this is not possible, a patient may go through a period of much suffering before he pulls himself together. However, he can usually reach some kind of satisfactory solution. The human organism has a way of re-establishing a level of adjustment for a degree of successful functioning.

In addition to unavoidable interruptions, there are some that may be avoided. I refer to the situation that arises when either the patient or the analyst decides to discontinue the analysis—particularly when the patient discovers that he does not really want to be analyzed. In order to forestall such interruptions and the concomitant feeling of failure on the part of the patient, analysts often start work on a trial basis. What is started tentatively need not be considered as a commitment. In this way both analyst and patient are free to reconsider the matter definitely at a later date. If a patient does not continue, he need not then have a sense of failure. Nor will he regard it as a rejection, should the analyst decide to discontinue treatment. Moreover, the analyst will be able to determine how serious the patient is about analysis and how much incentive for work he has. Such trial arrangements also give the analyst an opportunity to determine the severity of his patient's neurosis. If he finds that a long period of uninterrupted work is necessary, he may discontinue the treatment should future interruptions be likely or certain. Similarly he would be averse to working with a patient who could only come for short periods at intervals or who lived at some distance. The analyst would consider it unwise to upset the shaky equilibrium of a patient who might need help at any time. It would be better for the patient to continue functioning as he does or to wait until he could devote the time needed for his analytic work.

The question of interruptions may raise concern about the possibility of having to change your analyst. After a break in your work, your analyst might no longer be available. If you went to another city, you might be forced to choose a different analyst. Transfer to another analyst can often be advantageous. A second analyst brings to the situation a fresh point of view. He may see things that his predecessor overlooked. You will have had a chance to digest what you have learned about yourself and will bring to your second analyst the results of that work as well as additional observations you yourself have made in the interim. A change of analysts, far from being catastrophic or necessitating your starting "all over again," can be beneficial. Naturally, I am not advocating a change in analysts unless it is necessary.

It is understandable that people want to know if there are short cuts in analysis. A number of therapeutic techniques and procedures are used to shorten analysis. Only those frequently used will be mentioned here. There are many others that are utilized either alone or in combination with psychoanalysis. In view of the complexity of neurosis, it should be kept clearly in mind that their value is limited. Also, the effect of such therapy is frequently superficial and without lasting benefit.

Setting an arbitrary termination date—often limiting treatment to months—has been used as a technique for shortening analysis. The expectation is that the patient will be stimulated to work harder and that it will be possible to crowd many more insights into this short period. These insights the patient is to digest at his leisure after the analysis. This procedure may in a few cases, and under special circumstances, achieve limited success but as a rule it does not attain the purported objective. The patient does not really receive a short analysis; what he does get is a short period of analysis in which he receives superficial help with some of his difficulties, while most of them are left untouched. One danger of this technique is that the patient may be left with the notion that he has been completely analyzed. This may lead either to confusion, because he cannot understand why he is still so disturbed, or to the belief that he is now "completely adjusted" and can wear his analysis like a badge.

Hypnoanalysis, a method that combines the use of hypnosis and psychoanalysis, is at present receiving prominence as a means of shortening analysis. By means of this technique the analyst can gain information in less time than it would take were he to use free association. It is suggested that resistances can be by-passed while the patient is in a trance state. Under hypnosis, traumatic events in the patient's life can be recalled and re-experienced. The recall and re-experiencing of traumatic events may lead to a diminution in emotional tension. It has been claimed that hypnoanalysis hastens the therapeutic process because the analyst can use information obtained during hypnosis for interpretation when the patient is in his normal state of awareness. Whether or not an analysis is really shortened in this way still remains to be proved. The question is whether or not the information obtained under hypnosis has the same meaning as that obtained in a normal state of awareness because there is a difference between the analyst's having the information and the patient's realization of its significance. Rarely have I found difficulty in obtaining information. Almost always there seems to be enough information forthcoming; the difficulty lies in helping the patient to understand it. To me, hypnosis represents a distortion of the individual's faculties for participation and a distortion of a human relationship. It is my feeling that therapeutic work can best be carried on in an atmosphere that approximates daily living, namely in a state of full awareness and with the conscious and willing participation of both persons concerned.

Another short-cut procedure now being much discussed is narcosynthesis. Under the influence of a drug, such as sodium pentothal, the patient re-experiences certain life situations. This technique has been much used in the armed forces. The objective is to aid the patient to relive the painful experience and thus discharge his repressed feelings of anxiety and hostility in an atmosphere of security. The therapist then attempts to aid the patient to integrate—to synthesize—the information obtained. Just as in hypnoanalysis, the second phase of this procedure requires considerable knowledge and skill on the part of the therapist. Narcosynthesis has been reported to be of definite, though varied, benefit to many. According to my experience, its value is limited. The gains appear to come from the psychotherapy given and are no greater than the results obtained without the use of the drug. The basic validity of this procedure might be questioned on the same ground that hypnoanalysis is questioned.

Group therapy has also been widely used as a short-cut method. One of its values lies in bringing many more people into contact with psychiatry and psychoanalysis. It makes them more aware of their need for help and of the possibility of getting such help. Group therapy enables more people to get some treatment, though it is limited and often only superficial. For mild cases it sometimes appears to be sufficient. It has also been found useful as a screening procedure. Those patients who do not respond are regarded as sicker than the others and in need of more intensive individual treatment. The rapid rehabilitation of large numbers by one group therapist allows the other staff psychiatrists more time for the seriously ill patients. Analysts working with groups of less than ten and using the concepts of character analysis have concluded that clarification is still necessary regarding the details of the method and the selection of patients. They felt that the results obtained were limited. Frequently, however, members of the group began individual analyses and this outcome analysts regarded as one of the values of group therapy.

A large number of people are doubtful about the possibility of being successfully analyzed. Particularly, they question whether fear of crowds, homosexuality, insomnia, or other specific disturbances can be cured. Doubts as to the successful treatment of particular disorders may actually express a doubt about the effectiveness of psychoanalysis in general.

Such doubts often stem from a disbelief in the possibility of changing human nature. Usually when people say, "human nature is that way," they are thinking about the unpleasant and destructive things that men do. They are not referring to human nature but rather to distorted expressions of it. The following statements are representative of such attitudes: "There will always be wars as long as there are people"; "all human beings are greedy—if they weren't, they wouldn't be human"; "man is an uncivilized beast, otherwise he wouldn't need so many laws to keep him in check." People who talk this way are describing the manifestations of neurotic processes in emotionally unhealthy human beings.

What we regard as human nature may best be indicated by describing what is natural—that is, given by nature—and what is human—that is, what differentiates man from animals. Human beings, like all others animals, have within themselves, as part of their natures, a life or growth process. You can call it an urge, impulse, or drive. If this process is not impeded, the human being, like other animals, grows, expands, develops and relates himself to his physical environment so that he can obtain sustenance and protection, avoid enemies and defend himself against external factors inimical to that growth process. Man, like the animals, is born with certain endowments. However, he is helpless for a much longer time than animals are and therefore longer dependent on his environment—mainly on his parents. This gives him a longer period of time in which to develop the special resources he possesses—his erect walk-

108

ing position, the specialized use of his hands, his speech, and his reason.

Man because of his long period of helplessness and dependency on others in his early years needs, prefers, and is able to function best in groups. He can only become more of an individual as he relates himself better to others. Animals take from nature what they find and are dependent on its whims; man, on the other hand, can co-operate with nature for a more abundant and continued return. Man is the only animal that can foresee and plan with known ends in view. He has in a measure some choice about the future direction of his destiny.

Man has, from time immemorial, evolved guides for conduct expressed in moral codes, philosophies of life, religions and forms of government. These same values also appear in his ethics, in his art, music, and literature. They are expressed in his cultural behavior patterns throughout time. Certain social ideals have persistently manifested themselves as evidence of man's undying hopes and wishes. These may have been differently phrased according to the needs of the time or place in which they had significance. They have been expressed as the belief in the brotherhood of man, in the essential unity of all human beings, the importance of good will toward oneself and others, the true equality of all people, the right to respect one's own dignity and that of others, the importance of justice, and finally in the respect for man's productiveness whether tilling the soil or following intellectual or artistic pursuits.

109

Human nature has not changed since man first began living in groups. We cannot and would not want to change it. What we want to do is to free each individual of the neurotic encumbrances that stand in the way of his full development as a unique human being. No two people are born with the same vitality, temperament, or intelligence. What analysis attempts to do is to free the individual so that his innate qualities as a unique person and as a human being will not continue to be choked off, exploited, or wasted in neurotic distortions but will be available for free expression and full enjoyment.

It is on these positive qualities and constructive strivings that we count so heavily in analysis. People are not born with adverse emotional problems. They become destructive of themselves and toward others as a secondary consequence of destructive influences around them. The analyst's purpose is not to mold people or to attempt to impose upon them a pattern of living. His job is to help people free themselves of the neurotic obstacles that stand in the way of their natural growth. To attain this objective, he must identify what there is of health in the patient and fortify it.

What, then, is the source of this disbelief in the possibility of changing human nature or one's own particular nature? It derives from the conception that man cannot be an active and effective force in his own life and for his own betterment and this viewpoint, in its turn, stems from underlying feelings of hopelessness. The individual feels caught in the grip of insoluble conflicts. Because he is in conflict, his equilibrium is precarious and

110

he is in constant fear that it will be shaken. He naturally cannot feel secure even in the spurious harmony he possesses or feel sufficiently unified for constructive action. To such a person, change means a threat to his dubious equilibrium and the possibility of being thrown into the hopeless chaos of his conflicts.

Doubts about the possibility of change are sometimes expressed in questions such as this one: "Isn't my neurosis hereditary?" There is no proof that neuroses are hereditary. We do know that certain physical qualities are inherited from parents. Whether we inherit character traits or behavior patterns is doubtful. A neurosis is mainly the outcome of the adverse effects the parents' neurotic problems had on the child. The most significant evidence against the hereditary nature of neurosis is the fact that people with the most diverse heredities have been cured of their neuroses even where the family tree contained a large percentage of severe mental illness.

"How can I change when I was born that way?" is another form in which this doubt is sometimes expressed. It is true that at birth we all vary in our physical and psychological make-up. It is very doubtful, however, whether constitutional factors predetermine potential neuroses or effect a special variety of neurosis. Many physical and psychological qualities that had been considered constitutional or hereditary, or both, disappear during the course of an analysis. Moreover, people with all kinds of neurosis can be treated successfully.

Disbelief in an ability to change is often formulated in

111

a more sophisticated manner, thus: "If you say that my neurosis is due to environmental influences, how can you expect me to change while I continue to live in the very culture that made me that way? Where can I find the mythically healthy people you visualize; whom am I to emulate? Are you asking me to change the culture I live in? What culture can I use as a basis for comparison which will also act as a goal toward which I can strive and, besides, what can one person alone do against the world?" Actually, you do effect changes in your environment, just as you are molded by it. This interaction goes on constantly; it produces smaller and larger and at times even cataclysmic changes in the environment in which you live and in yourself. You do not have to initiate changes; they are inevitable and constant. Your task is to identify them and to direct the forces behind them into constructive channels.

True, your environment had its greatest molding effect on you when you were most malleable—as a child. But as an adult you are not dependent on your parents. You have developed more resources, greater independence, and a capacity for reasoning. With these capacities, you can use what is constructive in yourself and in the culture in which you live. Our culture, though deficient in many ways, is not completely destructive and inimical. It does offer a number of opportunities for real satisfaction and constructive development.

I am not acquainted with anyone who is completely healthy mentally but I do know a number of people who approximate that state and many more who are

112

moderately healthy. To me it is important to identify and co-operate with what is constructive in ourselves and in our environment, to work with those growth-favoring forces which are all about us. We can use as a basis for comparison those around us who are healthier than we are and, better still, our own increments of development. Satisfaction comes with the progress made by the individual's own efforts, from the very process of progress itself. The changes he sees in himself will be a stimulus to equal, if not exceed, what has been already accomplished.

"Don't you think I'm too old to be analyzed?" is one of the commonest expressions of a disbelief in the possibility of change. This attitude raises the question "How old is old?" A chronological criterion would be of little value because some people feel young at fifty and others feel old at fifteen. A person is and feels close to his actual age to the degree with which he is aware of and enjoys his emotional and intellectual maturity derived from experience. An exaggerated concern about physical health or an overwilling acceptance of emotional rigidity as a normal expression of aging might cause a person to forego an analysis because he fears his "blood vessels won't stand it." The feeling of being too old for analysis may be fortified and justified by the common cultural cliché "You can't teach an old dog new tricks." The truth is that analysts have worked successfully for some time with people not only of forty and fifty but also with those sixty and over. Not age, but the severity and the duration of the neurosis are the important factors to be considered. Naturally an older person has had more opportunities to develop a severe neurosis and more time in which a neurosis could become ingrained. However, one must also keep in mind that a longer life gives more opportunities for mitigating and ameliorating experiences and that often, with increasing years, comes satisfaction from worth-while tasks completed. Freedom may come with a lessening of burdens that fall to those who are younger. Age alone, then, should not be automatically considered a determining factor against analysis.

Some people are doubtful about the possibility of being successfully analyzed because of an underlying feeling of worthlessness. They are likely to ask, "Can I be analyzed?" or their feeling may be expressed more directly in the question, "Am I worth it?" They may state flatly, "I am not worth all that trouble." Such people may hold that others could benefit more from an analysis or are more entitled to it—indicating thereby the irrational value their feeling of worthlessness has for them. They may take an unconscious pride in their martyrdom, self-renunciation, or ability to manipulate others into analysis. Their sense of worthlessness may also force others to feel sorry for them, to do things for them without expectation of return. It may stem from a feeling that they have not fulfilled some irrational claims they have made on themselves. To the question, "Am I worth it?" our answer is "Yes. Every human being has worth and should have real significance in his own eyes."

114

The feeling that one is not intelligent enough or sufficiently well educated to benefit from analysis may be another expression of an underlying sense of worthlessness. Some people, simply because of a lack of information regarding analysis, may be under the impression that great intelligence and erudition are prerequisites to being analyzed. Neither is essential. A person can be analyzed even if his formal education has been very limited and even if he has a language difficulty. It is possible to communicate analytic interpretations to people who are illiterate. What is important is their good common sense. The feeling of worthlessness expressed in the notion that one is not intelligent enough or educated enough often springs from unconscious claims for superiority. People who demand of themselves that they should know everything and be brilliant on all occasions are frequently beset by fears and feelings of being stupid. Of course they are not judging themselves on the basis of their actual abilities and potentialities but rather according to irrational expectations. On the basis of such claims everyone would feel stupid.

An irrational claim for complete self-sufficiency causes feelings of worthlessness in some people. They look upon the neurotic need to be self-sufficient as a desire to be truly independent. They expect of themselves that they should function as self-contained units. Deluding themselves into believing that they can function in this way, they take irrational pride in what they regard as a virtue. They consider it a virtue to be able to do without— whether it be people, help, pleasure, or comfort. The capacity to endure the suffering they cause themselves they call courage and toughness. Such people feel that to consider and, worse still, to accept analytic help would make them feel worthless, weak, and self-indulgent. They are usually very susceptible to such slogans as: "A real man should be able to pull himself up by his own bootstraps"; "Control yourself, with enough will power you can lick it." Obviously such advice will only make the situation worse. The individual who already feels worthless because he is failing to attain self-sufficiency is told to flagellate himself along the same blind alley. Actually better advice would be to seek competent help to guide him out of his difficulties. Only by getting rid of irrational claims can one experience one's real worth and become truly independent.

Some people are doubtful about undertaking analysis because they are afraid it will harm them in one way or another. For instance, you may be concerned about what other people will think of you if you are analyzed. Adverse judgment about people who are being analyzed and about analysis in general is often expressed with apparent good intent; at other times baser motives may enter in. Since so many people still think that anyone who is mentally ill—that is, has emotional difficulties— is crazy, you may be considered insane for needing analysis or thinking you need it. Or your decision may be regarded as a stupid one: "It's a silly notion you have and you'll get over it," or "If you want to throw your money away, that's your affair." Some may express contempt and disdain: "You are weak willed"; "You take yourself too seriously"; "You're a sucker." Others may not stop at making derogatory comments but will do everything they can to dissuade you from going into analysis. Some will attempt to force you into stopping analysis if you have started and get you to try some of their pet cures. Quite a few people feel competent to advise others regarding physical ailments, but there are many more who think of themselves as expert in handling the emotional problems and the most involved psychological difficulties of their fellow men.

You may be legitimately concerned about other people's opinions but if you put off being analyzed because you are afraid of what other people might think, this may be an expression of your neurosis. Such a fear might indicate an indiscriminate need for approval or a fear of disapproval. Your associates may be implicitly or explicitly opposed to analysis; you may be afraid of their criticism. A neurotic need to conform may prevent you from rebelling. You may fear that the admission of your need for analysis will puncture your reputation as a well-balanced person in your own eyes as well as in theirs and will be followed by ostracism. The fear of being unable to have convictions and stand on your own feet, which you may experience as a fear of loneliness or isolation, may make leaning on others and clinging to them a stringent necessity. You would naturally wish

117

to choke off any thought or action of your own that might incur the displeasure of others without whom you feel you cannot exist.

Actually it is not the person who admits to having emotional problems but rather the one who does not who is in the indefensible position. Everyone in our society is more or less neurotic. The decision to be analyzed may be an expression of good sense, courage, and sanity rather than an evidence of fundamental weakness. It is debatable whether the persons who have "adjusted" to the demands of our sick society are not the sicker and the weaker for it. By adjust, I mean conform to standards and values which are definitely unhealthy—at the expense of true growth. So many "perfectly adjusted" people are not free, spontaneous, and creative. They are caricatures of what a truly alive person should be. They function like automatons who live by controlling themselves through will power and intellect, while squelching their real feelings. Neurosis may be an expression of the refusal to accept as desirable and laudable the ruthless individualism and competitiveness of our society. It would be my feeling that such a person should be respected for his tenacity in refusing to conform. He should be admired for his desire to seek help so that he may become a truly integrated person capable of co-operating with what is constructive in his environment and of working against what is destructive.

Your greatest security against adverse opinions about your analytic treatment will come from your own convictions about what you are doing. There may be times

118

when comments from others will prove annoying; some intrusions will be particularly unpleasant and difficult to handle. However, your irrational fears of others' opinions will be analyzed and you will find that what other people think can actually do you no harm. You can avoid much of this unpleasantness by regarding analysis as your own affair. If patients ask me or if the opportunity arises, I tell them to adopt this attitude. Such advice is often sufficient reassurance. Nor does it mean that you are encouraged to be secretive or surreptitious about analysis. You will have all you can do to handle your own emotional problems in connection with analysis. Discussing your analysis with others may only confuse and disturb you. Later on, when you are more certain of yourself, you will be able to answer the questions of those who are seeking legitimate information for themselves and you will not be upset by those people who, overtly or covertly, are bent on upsetting you.

You may be concerned lest analysis will upset your living arrangements, lest it will interfere with your friendships, disturb your professional life, or disrupt your marriage. What if, as a result of analysis, you do drop some of your friends? You may do this because in the course of the analysis you will find out that you really do not like them, that you have much less in common with them than you had thought, and that there are other people with whom you would prefer to associate. You may find out that they are not real friends but are continuing a relationship with you because you are useful to them or because either you or they have not had

119

the courage to break off the "friendship." If you drop them they may feel hurt at first but they may also be glad that you have taken the initiative in ending a relationship that was continued on false premises or through the sheer inertia of both parties.

You may fear that upsets which occur during analysis may disturb your working ability or even make it impossible for you to work at all. It is true that for shorter or longer periods you may not be able to work as well as you usually do, but this is not an unusual experience for any of us. As your analysis progresses and your general efficiency increases, you will be able to carry on with your work quite well and at a higher level than at your previous best, even though you may be quite disturbed at times. Where a patient finds it impossible to work at some point in his analysis, we often find that such an episode has occurred before. He may even have sought analysis because of that particular problem. Or his efficiency in his work may have been neurotically determined and kept up at the expense of other functions. When such patients lose the neurotic motivations for functioning like well-oiled machines, their drive to work naturally slackens at times and, as an overreaction, may even reach the zero point. When they resume work the basis is entirely different and their energies are directed toward obtaining satisfaction and pleasure in many other spheres besides their work. Such people, if they do not come to analysis, may break down suddenly and completely and under the worst possible circumstances. The reason why they crack up this way is be-

120

cause they drive themselves until there is no reserve left.

What about your fears that analysis may upset your marriage? Breaking any long and intimate relationship with a member of the opposite sex—or for that matter of the same sex—may cause serious repercussions. The breakup of a marriage, particularly if there are children, may be something almost too frightening to contemplate. Your fears lest your marriage fall apart may be quite legitimate; there may be a cooling in the relationship, obvious indifference, or hostility. Your fears might also be an expression of your long repressed doubts about the validity of the whole relationship. At times a strained situation can be relieved by giving a patient partial insight into a special problem or by making one or both partners see clearly what they are doing to disturb the relationship or what they are failing to do. If a marriage, which was well on the way to a breakup and possibly should not have occurred in the first place, terminates after a period of analytic work, the analysis cannot be considered the cause. All that can be said is that it may have hastened or postponed that separation for a longer or shorter period of time.

Occasionally a patient expresses fears regarding the possibility of a breakup of his marriage that turn out to be quite unfounded. In such cases, we find that fears relating to quite different problems were focused on the marriage relationship. The reason for this situation and the nature of the real fears must be worked through in each case.

My analytic experience with disturbed marital relationships has been rather unusual, as I have had the occasion to analyze husband and wife simultaneously in nine instances. I have also worked with just one partner of a number of unhappy marriages. This knowledge was amplified by discussions of the problem with other analysts. On the basis of my findings I can state that separations and divorces do take place in the course of and after an analysis. But so do engagements and marriages. We must ask: "Should a marriage be continued that ought not to have happened in the first place or that has become so disturbed that one or both persons are miserable?" It is my feeling that it should not if, in spite of the best efforts of both concerned as well as of friends and in spite of auspicious external circumstances, a happy solution could not be effected. If, in addition, one or both partners have grown during a period of analysis and become clearer as to what they want out of life and still persist in the desire for a separation, I feel that divorce would be the wisest decision.

Can a marriage be salvaged by analysis? Yes it can and, more often than not, it becomes a better one, particularly if it had been a pretty good marriage before. Analysis can make a good marriage better because it helps to eradicate frictions that come up so easily where people live intimately, as they do in marriage.

It is generally held that one analyst should not analyze husband and wife simultaneously but, as I have already mentioned, I have done so in nine instances. In each case both partners had severe neuroses. Their main

122

motivations for entering marriage were the unconscious expectations that certain of their neurotic needs would be fulfilled by the partner. It was only later in the marriage—not until they were analyzed—that this became obvious to them. They even found that they had glorified some of these needs and some of the partner's neurotic drives as virtues. They had not found the hoped-for solutions to their problems in marriage—that is, by living with or through another person. Tensions mounted, frictions increased, and an inordinate strain was thus put on a relationship that had already been entered into on so many false premises. Because of the mounting difficulties, whatever the partners really had in common did not have a chance to take root and develop. In all instances a break had been feared or contemplated on various occasions. It is quite possible that without analytic help most of these marriages would have ended in separation or divorce or would have continued unsatisfactorily. As it is all of them have remained intact and on a better basis than ever before with the definite possibility of steady improvement. How were these results effected? At no time was saving the marriage my prime objective; rather, it was to make clear to each of the partners what factors within themselves were disturbing the relationship. With such self-understanding and freedom they could avail themselves of their own resources and thus strengthen themselves as individuals as well as the marriage relationship—which in each case was what they wanted.

Some people fear that analysis will upset their religious faith or take it from them altogether. Similar fears are expressed concerning faith in a political creed, in a particular way of life, in a person—in short, in any kind of faith adhered to with religious fervor. The person who fears that he will lose his religious or other faith or that he will be proselytized in the course of his analysis may be fundamentally uncertain about what he regards as his convictions. In an earlier chapter, it was pointed out how doubts about oneself and about one's beliefs are the result of inner conflicts. The individual is divided, torn between the irrational pride he has in his neurotic drives and the real values he puts on what is genuine in himself. He attempts to achieve a feeling of harmony by making some sort of compromise. The inevitable result is that he cannot be wholehearted in his beliefs. Since he is not aware that the problem is in himself, his doubts about himself are expressed as fears of being influenced by others, and specifically of losing his beliefs and convictions.

Such inner self-doubt often causes people to cling to something external to themselves, for instance a church organization, a political party, an abstract dogma or creed originated by others and adhered to by a number of people, or to some one person.

People may have a certain faith to begin with because they were born of parents with similar leanings. They may have kept on believing because it gave them real satisfaction and filled a genuine need. But they may have continued in their faiths without genuine convic-

124

tion—from sheer inertia or because external circumstances or persons had not caused them to take stock, examine, and question. And finally, they may have selected a particular faith in exchange for another or for a number of others in succession, or as a haven of refuge. With this neurotic self-doubting are often associated feelings of helplessness and isolation that make leaning on a group, a person or an idea a stringent necessity. Because such people's need to believe and to belong is so necessary, their faith must be blind in order to allay their doubts. They use this blind faith to give themselves a spurious feeling of conviction which is turned into a source of irrational pride. The blind faith is then regarded as a virtue.

These people fear that what is neurotically motivated in their faith will be exposed. Such exposure will make it necessary for them to give up leaning on and clinging to others, to stand on their own two feet and to live by their own efforts. In short they will have to set out to find and develop a rational faith in themselves.

Nothing can make up for your genuine belief in yourself. You have the right to a genuine belief in yourself, just as you have the right to respect yourself and to believe in your own dignity as an individual. But you cannot have this attitude toward yourself unless you feel you have worked for it. It is interesting to note that certain oriental religions regard as the greatest sin, the sin of disbelief in oneself. Without a genuine belief in yourself you cannot have faith in anyone or in anything. Analysis can help you to revive and to regain your faith in yourself, strengthening what is genuine in your belief by dissipating what is neurotic.

You may fear that analysis will effect so fundamental a change in you that you will lose what you regard as your individuality. Analysts cannot and do not want to change your fundamental nature as an individual or as a human being. On the contrary, by aiding you in freeing yourself of neurotic difficulties, analysis helps you to realize your individuality and to develop your unique potentialities. It helps you to identify and develop what is positive and constructive in yourself.

Your fear that analysis will cause you to lose your individuality may have various unconscious, irrational causes. What you think of as your individuality may be your neurotic need to feel unique and superior. You may fear that analysis will rob you of such neurotic feelings which constitute your spurious individuality and will turn you into a mediocrity, that is, make you like everyone else. Being only human holds no fascination for a person who has unconscious illusions of grandeur about himself.

A special variation of this fear is the notion that analysis might deprive you of your artistic temperament and your artistic faculties. Analysis will not diminish or destroy either. If you have artistic abilities it will make it possible for you to develop them. If it turns out in the course of your treatment that you had illusions about such abilities, you and the world will be happier without them. Analysis of painters, designers, architects, and writers has shown that when their conflicts were resolved more of their energies became available for creative work.

You may fear that analysis will change you for the worse, that it will make you act in ways quite alien to yourself. More specifically, you may fear that it will make you selfish, egocentric, unfeeling, aggressive, hostile, or licentious. On the contrary, analysis will not make you that way, but if you do have such trends, analysis will bring them clearly to your awareness and help you to understand their meaning in order to do away with them.

There is, however, one concern that represents a more realistic evaluation of the analytic situation. You may be legitimately concerned about the emotional turmoil and pain that is a concomitant of the analytic process. There are ups and downs in every analysis; there are periods of discomfort and periods of relief. There will be times when you will be irritable, agitated or depressed. There will be other times when you will feel better, more effective, and more alive. If you are already quite disturbed emotionally, you may wonder whether you could stand becoming yet more upset in analysis.

There are a number of reasons for your becoming upset in the course of your analytic treatment. You may be quite disturbed emotionally at the outset and talk about it as though you realized it. However, full realization comes only later and, with it, the impact of how disturbed you really were initially. You may be upset by the interpretations you receive and the insights you get.

127

Awareness of the magnitude of the efforts necessary to extricate yourself not only from your present difficulties but also from those that have been accumulating before and since you came into analysis may also prove disturbing. And finally, you may be upset because of the decisions you will have to make and the radical changes you will have to effect once you have become aware that previous ways of living are no longer tenable or healthy.

As you get stronger, your tolerance of the painful periods will increase. Having experienced relief, and more relief as you get stronger, you will mind the painful periods less and less. Also, as your analysis progresses the pain will become less intense and the periods of turmoil shorter. Because you feel that you are getting somewhere with yourself and because you are seeing results, your attitude will become more optimistic. Your focus and interest will change. Instead of thinking stagnantly and maybe stubbornly, "Oh, how painful this is!" you will think "I don't like this discomfort. I'm going to find the causes for it and get rid of it." Naturally the analyst makes every effort to conduct the analysis with the maximum of efficiency and the minimum of pain, but a certain amount of discomfort is unavoidable. That is what you should expect and when you have lived through it, you will be the stronger for it.

You may fear that analysis will make you too introspective and ruminative. Such a fear may be due to a lack of clarity regarding the difference between constructive self-examination with the help of an experienced person, and destructive morbid introspection and

128

self-preoccupation. It is far better to examine doubts and fears about yourself in the light of genuine understanding than to live in a state of vague misapprehension and to attempt to bury or to deny such fears by a technique of flight or narcosis. An aversion to self-examination in the presence of another person may be due to a fear of exposure or humiliation, an exaggerated need for secrecy and privacy, an irrational suspiciousness. It may also spring from an underlying fear that people will think you weak for admitting that you cannot solve all your problems by exerting your will power, by disciplining your feelings through a mental effort. The purpose of analysis is to free you of those fears and to help you to develop a capacity for self-examination with the help of another person who is more experienced in this difficult task.

Some people have a fear of going insane in the course of analysis or because of it. They are usually people whose neurotic structure is so rickety and brittle that their equilibrium is upset by the slightest difficulty. They express their fear of loss of equilibrium, of things getting out of control, and of falling to pieces as a fear of going insane. This fear is a symptom of neurosis and disappears like any other symptom when the irrational factors that are responsible for its existence are exposed and dissipated.

However, in some cases the fear of going insane may be considered quite valid by the analyst. There may be a history of one or more psychotic episodes, or even if there has not been a previous breakdown, the patient may have been on the borderline of a psychosis on many occasions. By psychosis we mean that mental state in which an individual has lost contact with reality so that he no longer perceives himself or his environment as it truly is. His depressions or elations are out of keeping with the factual situation. Qualitatively and quantitatively a psychosis represents an advanced expression of what we see in a neurosis. A psychotic may regard his body or his person or others in ways quite alien to their reality. He may feel that he has no insides, that he is a superbeing and that everyone is a secret special enemy. He is judged legally insane if he cannot care for himself, if he may do harm to himself or others, if he does not know right from wrong, or if he cannot be considered responsible for his acts.

People who have had previous psychotic episodes or who have frequently been on the borderline of a psychosis may have a psychotic episode during the course of an analysis. The decision to analyze such patients, the manner in which it is to be done, and the circumstances all require the most careful and expert analytic judgment. Both the patient and those close to him must be acquainted with the risks involved. However, one should not overemphasize the immediate risks and overlook the possible long-range gains. The real question is whether the patient will become healthier over a long period of time even though his progress in analysis might be punctuated by psychotic episodes. Or in other words whether or not, in the end, the gains will be greater than the losses. The decision not to analyze such

130

a person also carries responsibilities. The patient may continue to have psychotic episodes without having had the benefit of analysis; worse still, his episodes might become more frequent and of longer duration.

In my opinion, the gains are greater than the losses in many such cases. Analysis may stave off further psychotic episodes. If analytic work is begun where a psychotic episode appears to be imminent or in an initial stage, that episode may be avoided or held off for some time. In the meantime much solid work can be done so that when the episode does occur it will be of shorter duration. Not only may analytic work shorten the psychotic episodes and lengthen the periods between them, but it may also make those intervals more worth while. Previous analytic work may also be of help to the therapist who treats the patient should he be hospitalized, for then the patient is already acquainted with the analytic procedure. The ultimate aim in the analytic treatment of such patients is to eradicate mental illness to the extent that psychotic episodes no longer occur, to enable the patient to grow and develop into a well-integrated person who can function on his own. This purpose has been achieved in a number of instances.

A number of people fear that analysis will make them too interested in sex, promiscuous, or immoral. Such fears may have been stimulated by the overemphasis on sexuality in Freud's writings; they may express the individual's unconscious fear of finding out that he has such drives or perhaps that he is indulging in sexual activities which he does not want interfered with. Such fears may

131

also stem from an unconscious prudery that may be obvious to everyone but the individual himself. His real fear may be not of becoming overinterested in sex but rather of becoming interested in sex at all. Such a development would interfere with his pride in his ivory tower existence.

Another concern, with the same Freudian background, is that the patient will or must "fall in love" with his analyst. This fear is caused by a misconception regarding the phenomenon technically referred to as the patient's transference reaction to his analyst. A patient can also "fall in love" as part of his transference in the same irrational way he has been "falling in love" before he came to analysis. You should have some liking for your analyst before you start working with him. If you come to like him more as the work proceeds that would seem to be natural and desirable and hardly a cause for concern—unless you had an irrational fear of coming to like anyone.

More often the fear of "falling in love" with one's analyst covers up a wish. The individual in that case is really more afraid that his love will be rejected than of falling in love. Such people would tend to fall in love with the analyst as they would with anyone else. For them being in love is a life condition. To them love should be able to solve all problems. However, to them loving means being neurotically dependent on the other person and demanding in return for this love that the burden of life be taken over. Such people will make the same demands on the analyst. With them, analysis can become quite

132

stormy when they realize that the analyst expects them to assume the function of living for themselves and that they must work for it.

Others fear that they will become dependent on the analyst, that they will feel incapable of making a decision without him or will become putty in his hands. They worry lest this dependence will cause them to prolong the analysis or that, having once terminated it, they will tend to keep returning for advice and guidance. If a patient has neurotic dependency needs, these needs will manifest themselves toward the analyst and will be analyzed. The fear of becoming dependent on the analyst may come from a lack of comprehension of the nature and purpose of the analytic process and a misconception of what true independence is. Being truly independent does not mean absolute neurotic self-sufficiency. It includes the ability and willingness to give and to receive help. Hence, returning for an occasional interview with your analyst might be an expression of true independence, common sense, and good faith. What would be more natural and rational than to ask for help from one who knows your problems, who has helped you free yourself of many of your difficulties, and who is skilled in giving just the kind of help you need? He would aid you in identifying and clarifying what is disturbing you at the time, indicate to you what progress you have made on your own, and point out the directions in which further work remained to be done.

Who Should Your Analyst Be?

HAROLD KELMAN, M.D.

WHY IS the choice of an analyst so important? Because so much depends on your relationship with him. This relationship will be an extended one in the course of which you will discuss with great frankness every aspect of your life, past as well as present, and will reveal facts about yourself of an intimate and often painful nature. It is of paramount importance, therefore, not only that you be in essential agreement with the basic tenets he follows in therapy and that you have confidence in him as a capable therapist, but that you have the utmost trust in him as an understanding person. Your belief in your analyst's integrity must go pretty deep to carry you through the trying periods of your work when you come to grips with qualities in yourself, of which you had not been aware and which you may find quite unpleasant to admit. You will share with your analyst a difficult task involving radical changes in yourself and you will often ask for and receive help from him.

Hence, choosing an analyst is a far more important step to take than selecting a physician. When you decide on a physician for the treatment of a physical ailment, his competence is your main criterion. His personality may play a limited role. But the success of an operation, for instance, is not much affected by the circumscribed personal contact between patient and surgeon. Once you have selected a physician, you put yourself completely in his hands. You ask for his help regarding certain specific complaints—usually of a physical nature. You answer all his questions, most of which concern your physical life history. If his examination reveals a physical disorder, he prescribes something concrete such as medicine. Your attitude is one of submission to a person in authority whose suggestions you may accept or reject. If you submit, the physician is responsible for the results; if you reject his suggestions or do not follow them correctly, the responsibility is yours.

The purpose and extent of a doctor-patient relationship are usually circumscribed, and its duration is usually short. Should it extend over a longer period of time, personal elements may enter into it to a larger degree. At no time, however, is the personality of the doctor explicitly regarded as a significant factor in the therapy.

From your analyst you expect help with your emotional difficulties. His questions relate not only to your physical history but to your life history as a human being. His prescription calls for mutual effort and responsibility leading toward a total understanding of the patient. The treatment is not only curative but preventive. It is growth-stimulating, too, and will help you improve your human relationships. To reach these objectives a relationship of an extended nature is necessary.

Since the choice of an analyst is so important and since neurotics are more or less indecisive, they often have difficulty in taking this final step even after they have already decided to be analyzed. In some, this indecisiveness may be quite marked and impede or prevent a final decision. Such people usually show the same indecisiveness in their work, in their social and personal relationships, and in their sex life. They are equally undecided about the selection of a mate, the purchase of a dress, or whether to have coffee with the main dish or with the dessert. At times this underlying agitation and uncertainty may be quite obvious; again it may be covered up by various rationalizations.

The main reason why such a person cannot decide is because he is compulsively driven by contradictory and irreconcilable trends. He is pulled in opposite directions; hence he cannot feel sufficiently unified in his aims to act decisively. A person who is thus driven exhausts himself. He may shuttle from one set of neurotic drives to the other or he may eventually succeed in giving his conflicting trends a spurious veneer of unity.

As a consequence of his indecisiveness, he may go from one analyst to another, yet never arrive at a final choice. Frequently he does a good deal of thinking and talking about this or that analyst without actually going

137

to see one. Very often the momentary decision to see an analyst leads to a phone call for an appointment that is not kept. This practice may go on for years. All analysts have had the experience of being called by a prospective patient who urgently asks for an immediate appointment and during the consultation informs the analyst that he has been "thinking about" analysis for a number of years. What he refers to as thinking is actually agitated or rationalized indecisiveness. Unable to decide on the right analyst, he may finally solve his dilemma by choosing a friend's analyst—not necessarily on the basis of that analyst's merits or on the evidence of real progress in his friend's analysis. To be "absolutely certain" he may wait until a number of his friends have successful analyses. Or he may think he wants to work with a particular analyst into whose office he then maneuvers a number of his acquaintances. Their satisfactory progress is to be the verification of his choice. Often much of this indecisiveness about choosing an analyst is really based on doubts about analysis per se.

Do such people ever get to the point of being analyzed? Yes, some do. They finally choose an analyst because their indecisiveness becomes so intolerable that they are forced to act. In this way, at least, they will give the impression of being decisive. They may rationalize such an action as a well-thought-out decision, and in so doing may succeed in convincing themselves and others that they are, in fact, really decisive. Obviously this is not a genuine decision but at least it gets them into analysis. They usually take the last analyst they saw, or the first one they can think of, or one that happened to be mentioned recently. External pressure in the nature of a life situation, or a friend's urging, may push them over the hurdle and literally land them in an analyst's office.

However some people never do reach an analyst's office, either because of indecisiveness or because of a state of chronic depression or elation or because of apathy or inertia. A person who oscillates between depression and elation may impulsively catapult himself into an analysis during his period of elation, knowing that he would not be able to do this once the depression sets in. In this way he hopes to ward off further periods of depression. A patient who chooses an analyst under these circumstances may be overoptimistic about his analytic prospects and will be disappointed later when progress is not as rapid as he thought it would be, but at least he does decide on an analyst who will give him the help he needs.

However, with those people who feel inert and apathetic, the chances of reaching the point of choosing an analyst are far fewer. They speak of themselves as lazy or as having limited vitality. They suffer from feelings of boredom, hopelessness, despair, and resignation. Such people do not feel themselves as effective forces in their own lives; they feel, rather, like helpless bystanders. It is difficult for them to initiate any action in their own behalf. The promptings of others may provide sufficient stimulus to carry them into analysis, but when the stimulus ceases they subside once more into a state of list-

139

lessness or apathy. They may then drop out of an analysis or continue with it through sheer inertia. Analysis in such cases must move very slowly because for a long period almost the entire burden must be carried by the analyst.

The choice of an analyst may be made unnecessarily difficult by questions which are culturally or neurotically determined and should be considered irrelevant in most cases.

Questions concerning the sex of the analyst are raised more frequently than any others. In the long run the sex of your analyst makes little difference as far as the successful conduct of your analysis is concerned. Whether the analyst is a man or a woman may be a pertinent consideration should you feel that analysis with one of the opposite sex would be inordinately painful or difficult. However, such considerations have only relative validity and should not deter you from making a choice where an analyst of the preferred sex is not available. In that case, analysis may be difficult for you for a time but whatever underlying disturbances are expressed in your attitude toward a particular sex will be worked through. You may find that your antipathy was exaggerated when you see how rapidly it abates. In fact, the reassurance that the analyst gives you on this score may be sufficient to make it possible for you to work together even though you have a strong dislike for the sex of your analyst.

140

You may prefer an analyst of one or the other sex because you have better and closer relations with persons of that sex. Because you feel comfortable in their presence and familiar with their ways, you may think that you will feel the same way about an analyst belonging to the preferred sex. And you fear that working with a person of the opposite sex will be just that much more difficult, especially if you have a strong antipathy toward members of that sex. Your attitudes toward either sex may have been significantly determined by your feelings toward your father and mother, or toward some other important masculine or feminine figure in your life. You may have felt loved or hated by either or both of your parents. Without being aware of it, you may have extended such attitudes to all men or women. Indiscriminate likes or dislikes of this nature are irrational and, if allowed to carry too much weight, may unduly influence you in your choice of an analyst.

Certain cultural attitudes toward men and women cause you to overemphasize the importance of your analyst's sex. You may consider so-called masculine and feminine attributes constitutionally determined or you may be quite conscious that they are culturally derived. Considering the multiformity of so-called masculine or feminine traits, one can easily make a case either for or against an analyst of either sex on this basis.

Some men prefer a woman analyst because they feel that women are more sympathetic and understanding than men; that women have motherly instincts; that they are kind, warmhearted, patient, affectionate, more

141

tolerant of human failings, and have a better understanding of suffering. They may fortify their preference
for a woman analyst by declaring that men are firm,
hard, and demanding; that they are impatient and insist on results without complaint even if there is concomitant pain and suffering; that they sometimes tend
to be brutal and cruel; that they measure other men by
their own concepts of pride, ambition, and success; that
their expectations of men are too high.

Some men, on the other hand, feel that they can work
only with men analysts. After all, this is a man's world,
they say, and only a man can appreciate masculine clarity, directness, and logic. And besides, they may add,
one can become a real man only by cutting away from
women's apron strings. Of women they say that they are
unrealistic and impractical; that they are too romantic
and sentimental; that they are not emotionally stable;
that they do not have as high a code of ideals as men
do; that they feel inferior to men, and therefore resort
to indirectness and deceit; that they are less competent
or intelligent than men are. Furthermore, they say, the
reason women seek careers is that they are frustrated
in love and a man would not want a frustrated woman
as an analyst.

Women may use similar arguments for or against an
analyst of either sex, but they do so from what is referred to as the woman's angle. Because most women
feel that their position is an inferior one or because they
feel that a woman's main role in life is marriage, they

142

frequently prefer a man analyst. What may be unconsciously operative is a contempt for women and an adoration and overvaluation of men and their position in society. There may be a neurotic need for a man's approval or a need to own and possess him. Consciously such an attitude is expressed by the cultural cliché that no woman is complete without her mate. Unconsciously there may be the feeling that life is only possible with a partner.

Analytic literature that you have read, or the type of analysis with which you have been acquainted, may cause you to attach undue importance to the sex of your analyst. Since sexuality is of major significance in Freudian analysis, the sex of your analyst would understandably seem of great significance to you. Moreover, since according to Freud, the outcome of analytic therapy is largely determined by the recovery of childhood memories, you may feel it desirable to have an analyst of the same sex as the parent with whom you were in greatest conflict or in greatest sympathy.

At times the presenting complaint itself may cause some patients to choose an analyst on the basis of sex. This is particularly true with men who are sexually impotent or ejaculate prematurely. Often they are adverse to going to a woman analyst. They have marked feelings of shame and humiliation. From a rational and cultural viewpoint this appears to be reasonable, for they cannot stand exposing to a woman their failure to live up to their notion of what a man should be. In analysis we often find this fear to be symptomatic of many other fears as well as a cloak for a general fear of exposure and for pervasive fears of being humiliated.

Neurotic motivations reinforced by prevalent prejudices often distort a patient's perspective in choosing an analyst. These motivations may relate to the analyst's nationality, his religion or his political belief; the focus may be on his native tongue, the shape of his nose or his party affiliations. Such prejudices always indicate and stem from disturbances in the patient's human relationships.

A difference in language background may sometimes be a relevant factor in the choice of an analyst. If a patient cannot speak English, it is understandable that he seek someone who is fluent in his native tongue because so much in analysis depends on verbal communication. All that is gained from the play on words, colloquialisms and tonal inflections would be lost, and consequently there might be misconstructions and misapprehensions on the part of both patient and analyst. However, the rejection of an analyst because English is not his native tongue rarely has a valid foundation. A foreign analyst would not attempt to practice in this country unless he was fairly conversant in the English language. The fact is that many foreign analysts have had a good education in English.

Nor is there any validity in the argument that differences in national origins between analyst and patient would make analysis impossible or at best very difficult. It is true that diverse cultures have varying effects on

144

the persons who grow up in them—to wit, the local and regional peculiarities evident in various parts of our own United States. But such divergencies constitute much less of a problem than a language block, and can be handled. Where there is a choice, an American or foreigner might do well to select an analyst of his own nationality and thus make it easier to accept analysis. But actually it will make little difference in the outcome of his analysis.

A patient who insists that his analyst speak his language or come from his cultural background would be doing so for neurotic reasons if the patient speaks English well and has adjusted himself to our ways of living. Similar irrational drives would be operative in an American who will have only an American analyst and who argues that his choice is made on the basis of patriotic considerations, contradicting thereby the true spirit of democracy which he believes he espouses.

Because of irrational fears of being identified with a minority group, a foreigner might select an American analyst to get a spurious feeling of belonging to a majority. An American might insist on a compatriot because he despises minorities, or he might lean over backwards to avoid facing his arrogance and contempt for people who are in a minority position, and select an analyst from that group.

All of these biased considerations in the choice of an analyst may be unconsciously motivated by general mistrust and suspicion, stubbornness, defiance, and arrogance. Or by an unwillingness to learn or change with a

145

consequent limitation and rigidity of viewpoint. They may also be due to a neurotic need to have everything one's own way or to bend others to one's will.

Both Jews and gentiles may prefer a Jewish analyst because they believe Jews can understand human suffering better, having suffered so much themselves. Actually, persons of all denominations have had their share of suffering and an analyst should be able to understand and be helpful to all patients regardless of their background or of his own. The assumption made by some Jews as well as gentiles that, because Freud was a Jew, Jews make better analysts is similarly unwarranted.

A Jewish patient may prefer having a Jewish analyst. Such a preference might be understandable if his Jewish origin has been a very important factor in the development of his neurosis. A Jewish analyst would be close to the patient's problem, and no time would have to be lost in explaining the patient's particular difficulty. An ingrained fear that every non-Jew is anti-Semitic may cause a patient to insist on a Jewish analyst. These should not be considered valid reasons for a Jewish patient to forego an analysis if a Jewish analyst is not available. In the analysis of such patients, it is frequently discovered that they place an exaggerated emphasis on the fact that they are Jews to explain many other emotional difficulties unrelated to that particular problem. The attitude may be an unconscious attempt to ascribe all of their disturbances to an external situation.

Political and religious prejudices frequently play a role in the choice of an analyst. When people display

146

such prejudices they are actually expressing the fear that their political bent will be considered a neurotic manifestation and that they will be proselytized. Though an analyst may be in sympathy with a patient's religious or political views, the patient cannot validly expect that he should be. Some persons go to the length of demanding that the analyst be an active adherent of the particular faith they profess. Such persons have become neurotically overfocused on one aspect of life and do not realize that the analyst is interested in them simply as human beings who are suffering. There have been instances where analysts have helped confirmed fascists, whose ideology they viewed with avowed antipathy, and so informed their patients at the outset. An analyst may tell you of his political affiliation and religious belief if it is a matter of great importance to you. But what should be of crucial interest to you is whether you believe he can help you with your emotional difficulties regardless of such beliefs. It is well to remember that if differences exist they are rarely absolute; nor do they exclude agreement on many other aspects of living. What is really important for you to know is that whatever conviction or belief of yours is solidly grounded will become strengthened in analysis and that only those of your leanings will be undermined that are based on neurotic premises. This should be the outcome regardless of the political or religious views of patient or analyst.

Concern about the analyst's political bent is frequent among communists. One of their arguments is that it would be disloyal to divulge party secrets to a person not belonging to the party or in sympathy with its activities. They must depend for their security on the universal and ancient oath that every physician takes not to divulge confidences made by his patient, nor to use such knowledge against him. Except for fascists, no person or group has ever challenged a doctor's duty never to repeat such information. If analytic scrutiny should reveal that what the patient held to be his firm belief in the communist cause is actually a spurious attempt to solve his inner difficulties and if as a result of this discovery he drops out of the movement, this can only be to his advantage as well as to the advantage of the party. This, of course, holds true of any political or religious cause.

Catholics frequently express concern regarding the analyst's religion. They fear that their belief will be undermined. What was said previously regarding irrational fears of losing one's belief is also applicable to this case. However, legitimate concerns in this regard might best be answered by a positive statement of what analysts of our school of thought believe. It might be called a psychoanalytic credo or philosophy of life. The following are some of its tenets; others are stated or implied throughout this book.

We believe that man is constructive by nature and becomes destructive only when his genuine urge to grow and develop has been frustrated. Naturally this is a relative matter. No person is completely constructive and rarely does anyone become totally destructive, absolutely inhuman. It is upon these latent constructive

148

forces in the patient and in his environment that we count so heavily to help him out of his difficulties. We believe, then, that man by his own efforts can free himself of the consequences of those inimical forces which made him destructive.

We believe that man has the capacity to seek and to find ways of availing himself of what is innate and original in himself and of enjoying its spontaneous expression. We believe that within the limitations of his natural endowment and those imposed and created by his parents, his culture, and his physical environment man can exercise a choice regarding the ways and directions of his self-betterment. We believe that man has the capacity to live according to the moral values of decency and respect for himself and toward others. We believe that man can have a rational faith in himself and that he can find solutions to his problems by means of co-operation with others. In short, we believe that people can live together in a truly democratic society and in a spirit of mutuality even though for the present, and for some time to come, the strongest stimuli moving them toward that goal may be a survival need and a fear of the consequences of the monstrous destructiveness created and unloosed.

Such a credo, though succinctly stated, has far-reaching implications. That this state of mutuality does not yet exist in the world need not cause us to despair. From time to time it has existed to some extent among groups and between individuals. It is a goal toward which we can aspire. When we are clear about our goal and have a

149

true humility about it, we will not have the fantastic expectation of seeing it reached in our lifetime. We will be able to obtain satisfaction from small successes and from some actual progress in moving toward it. With such a viewpoint we will be able to be more tolerant of other people's ways of reaching that goal since the ultimate objective is the same.

Having discussed a number of irrational and irrelevant factors that should not influence you in your choice of an analyst, I shall now suggest some criteria which may prove helpful.

You will want to know whether the analyst is a qualified practitioner. You can verify his official qualifications by consulting medical directories or by inquiring at the psychoanalytic institute with which he is affiliated. He should be a licensed physician who has served a medical internship of at least one year in a mental institution accredited for teaching. By the time he completes analytic training, he should have been satisfactorily analyzed by one senior analyst and have satisfactorily treated several patients, under the supervision of two other senior analysts. Usually, after a period of one to two years of personal analysis, an analyst in training is considered qualified to treat patients under the supervision of another senior analyst, and independently after he has been certified. He must have taken as part of his training a series of courses which as a rule extend over a period of three years or more. Actually, most analysts have far more than the matriculation qualifications and take much more work than is stipulated for certification by an accredited psychoanalytic institute.

It is important for you to know in what school of therapy the analyst has been trained. The psychoanalytic institute where he has trained and the psychoanalytic association of which he is a member, or medical directories will identify him with a particular school of analysis. You can obtain still further information by hearing him lecture, by reading the papers or books he may have written, and finally you might ask him what analytic theory he uses when you consult with him.

Some people hold that theoretical differences in psychoanalytic theory are ultimately of little import, but actually they are of very great import. The theory according to which the analyst practices is an expression of his philosophy of life. Your analyst's philosophy of life is important because it will influence you in the course of your analysis. It is inevitable that this should happen because you will be exposed to his way of thinking for an extended period. You will be influenced in your analysis, as you would in any intimate relationship of long duration. This does not mean that you will turn out to be a rubber stamp of your analyst's thinking. It is not important that you agree in details but you should be in agreement with the essentials of his view of life. It is inevitable that questions about human values come up quite frequently in the course of the analysis. The discussion of such questions makes great demands on any relationship. As it is, the load that the relationship must carry to fulfill its other tasks is already heavy. If agreement on essentials is lacking, the strain may be too great for the successful conduct of such a venture.

The particular theory the analyst holds is not only expressed in his attitude toward people but determines the nature of his therapy—what he will tackle in the analysis and what his objectives will be. A Freudian analyst for instance would be primarily interested in the patient's childhood and would spend much time in tracking down early life experiences. Our own main interest is in the actual character structure as it functions in the present. A Freudian analyst would explain many personality difficulties from the viewpoint of sexuality, while we would relate them to a person's disturbed human relationships. According to Freudian concepts, the desire to grow is narcistic—an evidence of something sick. We would regard such a desire as something constructive and healthy. These differences are indicative of the importance the analyst's theory has in therapy.

Whether the analyst is competent will be another vital consideration in your choice. You can judge this to some degree by hearing him lecture and by discussing his ability with those who know him or with people whom he has analyzed. He may be recommended by someone whose opinion you value. And finally, you may get some idea of his ability in an initial consultation with him.

You may want to know, in this connection, whether an analyst must be experienced in order to be competent. Experience in analysis is valuable as it is in any other endeavor or profession. It sharpens the analyst's perceptions and enables him to grasp problems more quickly, even though indications of their presence be slight. Experience makes him more deft in giving the necessary help for the solution of such problems. If, in addition to having learned from his practical work with patients, he has kept abreast of recent developments in psychoanalysis or even has made original contributions, you could not ask for more. However, the value of experience should not be overestimated. Analysts who have been recently trained and who are therefore less experienced have obtained the benefit of all that is available in psychoanalytic thinking to date. Then, too, native ability or gifts may make up in some measure for a lack of experience.

Age and experience are frequently thought of as going hand-in-hand, but this is not always true, either in regard to life experiences or in regard to experience in analysis. Since many physicians decide to become psychoanalysts only after having practiced in some other field for a number of years, it may often happen that a young analyst has more experience in analysis than an older one.

Cultural clichés can be selected to make a case for or against a younger or older analyst. Youth is filled with vitality, hope and optimism. Youth is in favor of change and of trying out new ideas. Youth has the originality and energy to handle difficult tasks—for example, analysis. But young people are immature, undependable and lacking in wisdom. And older people have the wisdom that comes from the experience of living. Older people have greater humility, are more tolerant, and have greater sympathetic understanding for human frailties and foibles. But they are rigid, fixed in their ideas, narrow in their interests and always looking backward rather than to the present and the future. Such argumentation is not only futile but also dangerous.

Actually, the age of your analyst is not of crucial importance. Both younger and older analysts may have vitality, curiosity, maturity, and wisdom. Undue emphasis on age is to your disadvantage, as is any one-sided and distorted weighing of the facts in attempting to arrive at a decision.

An analyst's reputation may help you in arriving at a judgment with regard to his competence. His reputation may be based on the books he has written, the lectures he has given, or his status in the organizations with which he is affiliated. You may want to select an analyst on the basis of his fame because you know so little about analysis and analysts, and hope that by selecting a famous analyst you will be getting one of real ability. Usually you will be right. However, you may do as well with an analyst of lesser reputation.

Reputation and large fees are often thought of together. A person may want to pay a large fee or the highest fee not only because he can afford it but because he hopes in this way to assure himself of getting a good analyst, possibly the best. In the field of analysis as in any other profession, it is to be expected that a person with great experience and a high reputation would command large fees. However, a person with less

154

experience and one whose fees are not so high may be equally competent.

There are certain cultural attitudes that favor an emphasis on reputation. The fallacious notion is fostered that fame and success must necessarily coexist with competence. The belief is encouraged that what is most expensive is best and that money can buy the best of everything, which is, of course, a fallacy.

An emphasis on reputation may be due to an irrational need to live by reflected glory. Hence a famous analyst may be sought out of a desire for prestige, a desire to be envied by others, and an expectation that the association with such an important person will bring with it special privileges. The person who feels he must have an analyst of superior reputation may really be seeking one with magical ability. He may feel that his difficulties are so great that only a superperson can help him; that only a superperson can give him the courage and faith to break away from whatever upsets him. He may expect from this magician a quick, painless cure that requires no effort on his part, no real attempt at change. Or he may feel that by reason of his own unique qualities he deserves such an analyst who will then endow him with superabilities.

Often what people are seeking is not a competent analyst but the perfect analyst to whom they feel entitled because of their own perfection. He is to help them realize this illusory quality. But the perfect analyst does not exist any more than the perfect patient.

The final criterion for your selection of an analyst will

be your feeling about him as a person. You should feel that you can trust him, that he has integrity, that he is an understanding human being who is interested in you and your problem—in short, that he is the kind of person you would like to work with. The way he thinks, the manner in which he goes about his work, and the nature of his relationship to his patients should appeal to you. Here again you can get some initial impression from hearing him at lectures, reading some of his writings, talking to his patients or other people who know him but, best of all, by talking to him in one or several consultations.

The reader may ask, "How can a neurotic person form an adequate and valid judgment of another person?" Is he capable, for instance, of realistically evaluating the analyst's competence? A neurotic is not a completely confused person. He is only confused in some ways. In fact, in certain spheres his observations and deductions may be quite astute. It is well for a person who is neurotic to know this. The knowledge will prevent him from immediately discarding all his judgments and will protect him from being deceived by his own confused reactions. It will help him to maintain a certain skepticism about his feelings and will give him an opportunity to examine them more carefully. In this way he will not be impressed too readily by the intuitive feeling he has about an analyst, nor will he too rashly discard his own intuition.

Furthermore, a person who is neurotic should not be too disturbed because he does not have a feeling of deep

156

conviction about his reactions or decisions. Although an attempt has been made in this chapter to define the criteria for selecting an analyst as clearly as possible, none are absolute. All are subject to error in the evaluation and in the weight they should carry. You cannot be absolutely certain that you are making the correct choice. No one can foresee or take into account all possibilities and eventualities. Such an expectation would be irrational. Certain risks must be taken. They are present in any decision or relationship. After having made an evaluation of your needs and goals and the evidence at hand, you must take a chance.

What Do You Do in Analysis?

ELIZABETH KILPATRICK, M.D.

DURING the evolution of psychoanalytic thinking the concept of the patient's role in analysis has been constantly changing. The greatest change that has taken place in conjunction with new theories has been an increase in the patient's share in the therapeutic process. When Freud and Breuer first began their explorations in mental catharsis the patient had to make no conscious effort whatever. On the contrary, he was reduced to passivity by being placed under hypnosis. It was not until a later stage, after Freud had discovered the value of free association, that mental activity on the part of the patient began to be encouraged. Thereafter, Freud and his followers urged their patients to mention all their thoughts, feelings, and impulses during the analytic session. This often necessitated deliberate effort on the part of the patient for it meant that he must work against the pressure of his own resistance.

Ferenczi carried this technique a step further: he required the patient not only to mention everything that came to his mind but also to act out his feelings and impulses. Both Freud and Ferenczi encouraged their patients to relive past experiences during the analytic hour but Ferenczi introduced a new element: he insisted that the patient deal with the analyst not only as someone who represented a figure in his past but at the same time as a person in his own right. This development opened the way to a more natural, matter-of-fact relationship between patient and analyst and placed the patient in a position to take responsibility for his own attitudes and behavior. Present-day analysts continue to encourage the patient's mental activity in analysis; and therapy as it has now developed demands alert, intensive work on the part of the patient as well as the analyst.

This emphasis on shared responsibility constitutes without doubt the most significant of the changes in the patient's role in analysis. It recognizes the patient's ability to exert himself in his own behalf and, even more important, it recognizes the existence of an incentive toward development and growth. Our concept of neurosis takes full cognizance of the extent to which neurotic trends hamper the patient in his striving toward inner freedom, and we see the task confronting analyst and patient as an analysis of the entire character structure. During the analytic process we see the patient becoming capable of directing his energies more and more surely toward the active solution of his problems and moving toward the realization of the potentialities which he actually has. This form of therapy assumes the right of every human being to choose his way of life. It also assumes a capacity for internal change and an ability to discard even the most cherished habits of thought and feelings in the interest of larger growth.

Under these conditions, as you begin analysis you may well anticipate important modifications in your view of life and people and in your basic personality. You should know that not only your behavior will be different but that your feelings will be different as well.

This does not mean that you will be forced to accept anything you do not believe about yourself or to become anything against your will. It means rather that you will be helped to see the functioning and the consequences of unconscious neurotic forces around which your life has taken shape, and that you will come to appreciate how hopelessly they defeat the possibility of a satisfactory life. Your objective, then, will be to work spontaneously toward elimination of these forces in order to have more energy available for purposes constructive to your development.

After you have selected your analyst and before you actually begin analysis, there will be practical details to settle; these involve mutual agreement and lay the foundation for your partnership. Your fee is one of these, for it should be realistically determined with full fairness both to the analyst and to yourself. In response to subjective needs you may attempt fee plans that are unworkable or unjust. For example, a patient may be under

161

the impression that if he makes a financial sacrifice he will progress more favorably. Or, on the other hand, he may have a sense of demonstrating strength if he arranges to pay less than circumstances warrant and so seemingly get the best of the analyst. Neither approach is sound. Both would be indicative of neurotic needs and as such would be, necessarily, material for analysis in time. Consequently the one essential is that all possible mutual clarity be brought to bear and that the first discussion of the fee will be approached with all the honesty and sincerity you can command. Your analyst knows, of course, that some of the factors that determine your decision lie beyond your awareness at that time. He certainly will not hold you to any rigid standard. He may even suggest some reconsideration of the initial agreement at a later point.

The same principle applies to any advance agreement with regard to broken appointments. You will be asked to assume a measure of responsibility in this area, too, even though it is fully understood beforehand that your emotional needs may cause you to disregard some of your planned visits with the analyst.

You will want to bear in mind as you start out that, generally speaking, your analysis is a private affair between your analyst and yourself. You may, however, find yourself experiencing a compulsive need to talk about it excessively or, on the other hand, to keep it unduly secret. Do not worry if you do. No great harm will follow either course and, as you would expect, both attitudes will come in for examination at the proper time. The same is true of your desire to read intensively in psychoanalytic literature. Do not take this too seriously. At times you will find that your reading clarifies some phase of your analysis; and there may be other times when it interferes. A good rule to follow is that you should try to understand what you really want to get from reading. Is it a clearer insight into your own perplexing problems or are you trying to fortify yourself against making a realistic approach to these problems by making them seem theoretical?

The frequency of your analytic sessions may vary, but will be agreed upon tentatively at the outset. The number of weekly sessions will depend on what the analyst considers to be your individual need. If you come with an acute problem, the analyst will prefer to see you daily in the beginning. And later, although he may see you less frequently, you will find him ready to temporarily increase the number of your visits if you need it and if he can make the time available. Other considerations enter in. Patients differ in the rate at which they can work and digest help; some do better with longer intervals between appointments. Although it is true, as mentioned elsewhere, that it is generally advantageous to have four or five analytic sessions a week, patients who come less frequently or have treatment intermittently have been successfully analyzed. This is a point to bear in mind in the event of obstacles presented either by distance from the analyst, finances, or limitations in the amount of time that you and the analyst have available.

163

The usual procedure during the analytic session is that you lie on a couch, while the analyst sits in a chair behind you. This arrangement generally affords the patient maximum opportunity to relax and concentrate on himself; he is less influenced by the analyst's presence than he would be otherwise. Your analyst will not assume any inflexible rules regarding the use of the couch, however, and may find it advisable to make modifications to suit your individual need. Some patients, at the beginning of analysis, feel apprehensive about what may happen to them and are tense and uncomfortable unless they can watch the analyst. Others are so detached that the unusual position heightens their sense of unreality to the extent that they do not feel part of the experience they are going through. If for these or other reasons the arrangement is disagreeable to you, you should feel free to move about or sit in a chair. The most important consideration, however, is that you mention your reactions to the situation at once; for in this way you make your individual attitudes available for analysis. If you are to derive benefit from your analysis, you will hold steadfastly to a determination to be frank, honest, and sincere with yourself and the analyst throughout.

Analysis is a growing experience for a patient. During your analytic sessions you will visualize goals and work toward their attainment. Briefly these goals are: becoming acquainted with yourself as you are (not as you think you are); understanding your particular con-

164

scious and unconscious attempts at solutions of problems which confront you; evaluating these solutions and their effects on your life; changing conditions in your personality by resolving neurotic conflicts; and, when your real self has become free, mobilizing your resources in directions of your own choosing. You will work toward these goals more or less simultaneously; while becoming familiar with one part of your personality, you will be engaged in evaluating another and changing yet another. For purposes of clarity I shall describe these processes as though they were dealt with one after the other.

Your first objective will be to know yourself. You will say: "But I do! I know a great deal about myself." This is true but the knowing of yourself through analysis will be quite different. It will mean a more thorough knowing, and a knowing about your motivations. It will mean becoming acquainted with and experiencing as part of yourself all your conscious and unconscious attitudes toward life; what you think about yourself and about other people; your feelings about your background, your past experiences, and what you are doing now; what your fears, your hopes, and ambitions are; how you think, how you come to decisions, and what you do about them; your dreams and your phantasies, the things which make you happy, irritable or sad. You will learn of the factors which determine your mode of life, and the way you meet difficult situations. At first you will come to know the things you are aware of to some extent already, then those you have vaguely suspected, and from time to time you will learn about elements in yourself that are quite new and foreign and that you may have difficulty in accepting.

The process by which this comes about is free association. It consists in relaxing, and letting your thoughts speak for themselves as they arise. This is not quite as easy as it sounds. You will have difficulty in always being frank, especially at the beginning when you have not yet become familiar with your analyst. You may have doubts and may question the importance of mentioning everything you think. Your thoughts may seem irrelevant and disconnected. Such doubts and hesitations should all be brought into the open as part of the associations. They tell you about yourself. As you associate, you will notice changes in your mood, and at times will be anxious or irritable. It is important to talk about these reactions too. They give a clue as to which of the associations are more significant, and thus open the way to discovery of your values and standards of life. You may begin a session by talking about your past or present life, or by commenting on your thoughts at the moment. You may give, like an onlooker, an account of everything that has happened to you since the last session, or you may go on with a more or less continuous story, session after session.

What you discuss and the particular way you go about discussing it will be different from the way in which any other human being would proceed. The important issue is not what you talk about but what information you gain about yourself in doing so. Some of the first advantages of your analysis will be that you are free to say anything that comes into your mind, to ask the analyst's assistance, and to let him know your reactions to the way he goes about helping you. Quite early you will begin to notice and to comment on what you are doing and saying. You may find that you cannot talk as freely in analysis as you do elsewhere and that you have difficulty bringing up certain topics. This may be due to the presence of the analyst or to the nature of what you intended to say. In either case you should subject your hesitation to further scrutiny. Unless you go into the cause of these little hesitations each time they occur, they may extend to silences of several minutes, or to a whole session or even the greater part of several sessions.

Struggle against going where your associations lead may be indicated by abruptly changing the subject, jumping from one thing to another, or not listening to what you are saying. When you let the analyst know what is going on he will help you to uncover the resistance and to deal with it. You may come to the session in a cheerful mood, and find yourself becoming tense, anxious, or irritable. Again, you may feel a burden lifting as you talk. You may relate these changes to something that happened before you came, to something the analyst has said or done, or to something you have said about yourself. By attempting to understand all these occurrences, you begin to take responsibility for your share in the analysis. By relating the variations in productivity, the mood changes, and the content of the associations, you will realize what is of importance to

167

you and what makes for happiness, fear, or dissatisfaction in your life.

As you talk about your associates you will indirectly disclose the manner in which you meet life situations as well as the values you place on certain human qualities. At first you will find yourself attempting only to analyze the motives and attitudes of others, convinced that yours are the natural reactions to what is happening around you. In time you will begin to see yourself emerging as a definite personality motivated by individual wishes and desires, responding to other people and dealing with situations in ways peculiar to you. You will rightly suspect that you take a definite part in determining what happens to you and will begin to ask such questions as, "What did I do that permitted me to be taken advantage of?" "I want this woman to love me; what am I giving in return? What am I willing to give?" In short you begin to look inward for reasons for your behavior as well as outside yourself.

A patient said recently: "It is no use dealing with labels. I don't know what kind of a person I am and I must let myself tell me." As you assume this responsibility you begin to discover that you are engaged in fulfilling many special needs that you were unaware of. You find that you have many rigid attitudes. You may find that you are in a chronic state of indecision. As you hesitate, someone takes what you realize later you wanted, and in consequence you feel irritated and resentful. You may wish to have friends but find you are unwilling to share your feelings or your efforts. You may hold yourself responsible for every misfortune or place all the blame on the other person. You may be attempting to gain your purpose through passivity and avoiding all responsibility.

A patient may come to analysis with the idea that certain characteristics are interfering with his life and find through associations that others, previously hidden, are more detrimental. For example, a patient complained that he was so compliant that everyone took advantage of him. In this state of feeling abused he spent several sessions talking about other people's shortcomings, emphasizing how various situations should have been handled, and criticizing others who had opinions which differed from his. Meanwhile he pushed aside all the analyst's suggestions to listen to what he was telling about himself in his associations. Soon he began to regard the analysis as another of those situations where he was being taken advantage of as he felt he was getting nothing from it. When he was able to deal with his expectations here, he began to realize why he felt life to be so threatening. He saw himself as a person with grandiose notions about his ability who felt it was the analyst's function to show him how to make others recognize him as superior to them. In the light of this insight his feeling of compliance and being taken advantage of took on a different significance.

Such disclosures may cause you some discomfort. Some of the things you liked about yourself are not standing up well under scrutiny. It is disturbing to realize that you have characteristics you did not know about

169

and the thought that still others may come out is alarming. You may begin to feel sick, humiliated, angry, or frightened. You may feel unreal and not understand what is being said. These are evidences of anxiety which invariably occur during analysis when a patient comes upon unacceptable truths about himself, and later when he is faced with the necessity of doing something about them. You may be able to disregard the discomfort and push through to greater clarification, and the anxiety will then diminish.

Or you may unconsciously attempt to relieve the anxiety by doing things that are unrelated to your current problem in analysis. This is called resistance. It becomes apparent in many ways. You may deny what you discovered about yourself. You may try to neutralize it by talking about other characteristics. For example you may have come upon evidences of cruelty in yourself and begin to talk of your helpfulness to others. You may discover that you have a headache or begin to worry about an old physical ailment. You may remember something unrelated but urgent that you must talk about. You may become absorbed in thinking of others less well adjusted than yourself. You may even become dissatisfied with the analyst and the whole analytic process and wish to discontinue. If you are to make progress, it is your task to be on the alert for these attempts at escape and to enlist the analyst's help in your struggle to overcome them.

In describing everyday activities your selection of the things you discuss in detail or omit will be significant.

170

For example you may concentrate on your work because you are successful there and wish to emphasize only your successes. Or you may feel apart from people and try to find in your work the satisfaction you cannot get elsewhere; or you may be using it as a way to get closer to people. Again you may be looking for reassurance or help from the analyst. You may bring up only situations in which you have failed, have been unfair, or have hurt someone. Whatever you talk about will be used as a medium through which you gain access to your conscious and unconscious motivations and, as these are elaborated upon, you come to understand their real value to you.

You may be wondering at this point, "But how do I get at my unconscious?" There is no wall or chasm between the conscious and the unconscious, and as you successfully master the art of free association by overcoming resistances, your unconscious will be readily accessible. Sometimes unconscious material comes to the surface through associations with dreams, with a snatch of song, sentence, picture, phantasy or old memory which recurs quite unheralded.

As you talk of the people whom you like, dislike, admire, emulate, or quarrel with, you will gain insight into human values and standards. You may admire a person because he has characteristics you admire in yourself. You may be blind to or intolerant of undesirable qualities in others which you have but do not recognize. You may sympathize with and expect less from an associate because he has characteristics you recognize in yourself,

171

and are unable to change. You may resent someone who has succeeded where you have failed, and be unaware of your reason for disliking him. In short, many of your feelings and attitudes toward your associates are subjectively determined.

Although your relations with friends give you an opportunity for disclosing and evaluating attitudes which disturb interpersonal relationships, your relations with the analyst will serve this purpose even better. In spite of your conscious realistic appreciation of the analyst as a physician, and your determination to stick to your purpose of dealing with your problems during analysis, you will become involved emotionally with him. As in all human relationships your unconscious needs will affect what happens between you. The patient-analyst relationship is intense: first, by reason of the especially intimate nature of the work and, second, because there is actually so much more at stake than in other relationships. You are sharing with the analyst responsibility for something that involves your whole future life and happiness. You will share in this partnership in a way that is representative of your life as a whole.

Since the analyst is much less involved emotionally than your family and friends, you will be able to see your attitudes, desires, motivations, and sensitivities in a more neutral setting. For example, you may have compulsive needs for affection and approval which will be shown in seeking the good opinion of the analyst, in wanting to be his best patient, in wanting to be singled out for special favors and protection. You may want to

172

draw the analyst into social activities and may feel rebuffed when he does not accept your invitations. Some patients have phantasies of a love relationship or even marriage with the analyst. Hostile, aggressive drives are shown in wanting to argue and fight with the analyst, in suspicions of antagonistic attitudes in the analyst, in disparaging and belittling him, in challenging and forcing tactics, in refusing help, in overlooking his considerateness. Tendencies to withdraw emotionally are shown in cold, aloof attitudes toward the analyst, in wanting to keep everything on a cold, practical basis, in attempting to exclude any mutual exchange of feeling. You may choose a passive role and expect the analyst to assume all the responsibility—to tell you what is wrong with you and what to do about it. You may even ask him to tell you what to talk about.

These are some of the manifestations of neurotic behavior in your relations with the analyst which will gradually become apparent to you. You will attempt to deal with him in a certain way at one session and quite differently at the next one, all in accordance with how you feel or what you think he is doing to you or thinking of you. One of your important tasks in analysis is to keep aware of such fluctuations in your attitude toward the analyst and to work toward reducing the intensity of subjective reactions that interfere with co-operative effort.

Many of your associations will concern events from the past. From these you will discover that certain attitudes have existed for a long time. You may have avoided emotional involvements for years; you may have consistently shunned responsibility, or you may not have been able to get along with others unless they did exactly as you wished. With your present knowledge you will understand why you have always experienced difficulties in certain situations, how you have alienated others or been unfair to yourself. Awareness of the part you have played in your life and of the length of time you have been moving in wrong directions will give you a feeling of optimism about the effect of working in another direction, as well as more patience with the long, involved process of analysis.

As you review your childhood at long range, and with an awareness of your own strivings, you will get an objective viewpoint for the first time of the adults in your early life. You will see them pushed by their own hidden striving and in consequence neglectful of the rights of you—the small child. You will come to understand the stresses you were subjected to, and to realize how you were driven into adopting devious ways of getting along. As you continue to follow yourself through life, you will see how devious ways led to more complications until you were deeply involved. This will help you to assume responsibility for your share in what you have become.

Dreams are frequently recalled during an analytic session; they are a valuable aid to the patient in gaining an insight into his unconscious fears, hopes, and the solutions he is attempting to reach in his everyday problems. They are of particular value to a patient who finds it difficult to talk about himself. The way you deal with

174

your dreams in analysis will be characteristic of the way you undertake any project. You may forget them. You may have such long dreams that the following analytic session is occupied with recalling them. You may take full responsibility for interpreting a dream or you may leave it entirely to the analyst. An investigation of these attitudes will increase your self-knowledge.

To benefit from dream analysis you should know that your dream is peculiar to you, and that the content is correctly understood only when interpreted through your associations. Ideas and feelings are frequently disguised in dreams by symbols, and these too become meaningful only through the dreamer's associations. A dog, for example, may be a symbol of a friend to one dreamer and an enemy to another. Your characteristics may be symbolized in various ways—frequently by other persons, animals, trees, boats, or houses. One patient had several anxiety dreams in which she was trying to build an enclosure to house many wild and domestic animals. The central figure in your dream will be yourself in some form, or some person or object representing a characteristic in yourself which you are ready to talk about.

Your dream associations may lead in different directions. As with all other associations, the path to follow is that which leads to a better understanding of yourself. They frequently reveal the discrepancy between your conscious behavior and unconscious wishes. A young woman, who was consciously eager to gain an understanding of herself and to take whatever help the analyst

175

could give her, began a long stormy analysis by relating the following dream: "Two women were fighting for the royal blue robe." Her associations were scattered and she was obviously uncomfortable. Some time later she disclosed her apprehensions about analysis and her fear that the analyst would rob her of unusual qualities she believed she possessed.

Dream associations may throw light on how a patient is unconsciously dealing with a problem in analysis. The following example illustrates how an outwardly compliant, pleasant patient discovered some of her real motivations. She dreamed that a salesman was fitting her with shoes which were as broad as they were long. While she kept encouraging him to show her more shoes she was saying to herself, "I won't wear any of them." Her associations led to hidden feelings about herself and indicated that she believed she had most unusual qualities. She discovered that she actually did not wish to have anything to do with anyone unless she could dictate the terms. She also discovered her need for approval. She would have liked to frustrate others' attempts to secure anything, but was afraid to do anything overt because she was afraid to have anyone dislike her. Her solution was to appear compliant but to detach herself and remain unconvinced. By this maneuver she was able to repress hostility which was aroused when she did not have her way, to maintain her unrealistic belief in herself, feel loved, and secretly enjoy the satisfaction of seeming to have defeated the other. It was most help-

176

ful for her progress in analysis to realize that she was contemplating these tactics toward the analyst.

As analysis proceeds the patient is rewarded for his sincere searching and frankness by a clear revelation of himself. He will discover many qualities he likes and will wish to cultivate. He will become aware of more and more attitudes that are making life intolerable. He sees himself ineffectual in work because his attention is divided. He finds himself striving to attain certain goals only to be dissatisfied when he reaches them. He finds he is irritated because he does so much for others and when he does something for himself he becomes panicky. He recognizes his contempt for himself and his hostility toward his fellow men. He attempts to change but soon finds himself back in the old pattern. There is no real progress until he makes the significant discovery that many of his attitudes exist for the purpose of complying to neurotic trends. Because of this he is unable to change them through will power. His whole pattern of living is beyond his control. He finds he is continuously compelled to follow the dictates of inner drives that are often at variance with his best interests. He is in conflict between what he wishes to do and what he feels he is driven to do. He is indecisive or leaves the decision to someone else. As a result of either solution he is anxious, depressed, or tired much of his life.

During analysis he will discover that many attitudes have developed in the service of one neurotic trend. He may find, for example, that in order to serve a compulsive

177

need to be always superior he cannot take an inferior role. He cannot learn, but must phantasy that he is better informed than others. He must avoid all criticism. He must always feel in control. He pushes or wheedles others into agreement with him. Accomplishment of these purposes brings relief. But the very nature of the neurotic structure makes the relief temporary, and he is driven to greater and greater lengths to get similar satisfaction.

Another group of attitudes serves a different neurotic trend operating simultaneously with the first, and the patient sees himself frantically attempting to serve two masters, making compromises that involve him more deeply. He becomes hopelessly lost in confusion and anxiety. By analyzing his behavior—not only in his everyday activities but in the analytic situation itself— he comes to see the devastating effect of his compulsive, conflicting attitudes. They exhaust him, divert his energies, and make him ineffectual.

Eventually the patient comes to realize that the goal of his analysis must be the elimination of the neurotic trends which motivate his attitudes. Without this there can be no relief from the neurotic pattern of living.

The first part of this task is identification of trends. This is accomplished by constantly evaluating attitudes and determining the unrealistic neurotic purposes they serve. It will be found that there are many groups of conflicting attitudes, and that each group serves a particular neurotic trend.

Another important step is coming to recognize a trend

178

as an integral part of your personality for which you are responsible, to evaluate it, and to experience it functioning in relation to other trends. A good illustration of this is that of a patient who recognized his dependency but took responsibility for it only as he saw it resulting in unsatisfactory relationships with other people. He made many attempts to get rid of one person after another on whom he was dependent. But each time he disposed of one host he would adopt another. He made no progress until he recognized that he was compulsively driven to pass the responsibility for his life over to someone else, and in return to serve that person. No relationship could be satisfactory on such a basis. He made further progress when he evaluated an equally strong need, operating simultaneously, to regard himself as set apart and possessing most unusual qualities.

A further step is the important one of becoming conscious of and evaluating the trends with the ultimate objective of disposing of them. This will be accomplished by analyzing their functions and consequences everywhere they are found operating.

Your relation with the analyst, which you found so helpful earlier in isolating your attitudes, will be even more helpful now in resolving neurotic conflicts. Evidences of conflicting trends are continually becoming apparent in this relationship. For example, you may be evaluating your need for power and the analyst can point to specific times when this need has made you disrespectful toward him. During one session several trends may be seen in operation. You may attempt to please

179

him and thus win his approval. You may demonstrate your need for control by having anxiety when he points out something you failed to recognize. You may feel temporarily successful by misleading him and thus exploiting him. You may strive to demonstrate independence by rejecting all his suggestions. The laboratorylike atmosphere of the analytic situation is ideal for arriving at an awareness of what you are doing, of then understanding how unrealistically you are forced to behave and how impossible it is for you to achieve any measure of success or satisfaction while following these trends. Such insights furnish an incentive to give them up.

Your dream associations will again be helpful here. Although you are sincerely making a conscious effort you frequently find yourself blocked by an unconscious struggle against exposure. You become anxious. At this point you may have a dream that will provide a clue. Your associations will expose new material relative to trends or evidences of hidden resistances against insights you seem to have accepted. In this way extra tools become available for your work of resolving conflicts. A patient, who was very intolerant of any shortcomings in himself, felt he was able to give up his grandiose notions of himself after a brief evaluation of their effects. After this decision he dreamed: "I was sliding down a ramp and got stuck. Someone came to help me and I found I was not stuck at all—just holding on." His associations revealed his fear of giving up his high opinion of himself lest he would slip to the bottom and others would injure him. He was badly off because he was only pretending to be high and was in constant fear of being found out and punished. From this he went on to talk of the deceptions he used in order to feel that he was fulfilling his need to be superior, and how he hated people for forcing him into these deceptions. He felt they should simply accept him as superior without question.

The subjective value of these trends will be so great that every insight into their nature is followed by anxiety; and premature attempts to disregard their dictates are often followed by real panic. The patient is quite positive in his belief that he cannot exist if he fails to meet the demands imposed by them. He has depended on them so long he feels he will go to pieces without them. The struggle to free himself often produces mental states of hopelessness, depression, irritability, detachment, or inertia. He may become antagonistic toward the analyst for exposing a condition which he feels cannot be remedied. He may develop psychosomatic symptoms—sometimes becoming quite ill physically and feeling sure the whole trouble is organic. But when the anxiety abates he recovers physically. With each new insight the hold of the neurotic trend is loosened. Each advance is preceded by anxiety, then struggle. As more and more freedom is attained, incentive increases, more anxiety can be tolerated, and the work goes more quickly.

The intricacies of the neurotic structure are such that the patient cannot deal with a specific trend simply by isolating it, evaluating its importance to him and its consequences, and then discarding it. For in the process he invariably finds another trend that must be clarified before he can proceed. A small area isolated from an analysis may clarify some points regarding the patient's feelings and how he goes about extricating himself from conflicting trends.

A woman patient reported: "A woman in my club, whom I do not like, asked me to make an effort to remove the president of the club whom I do like, but who is not the best president in the world. I gave many good reasons why I did not wish to, but finally said, 'It is against what I believe but I'll do it.' I just couldn't help it. Later, when I talked with two other members, they said they would have nothing to do with it. Gradually it dawned on me that I was doing something no one else would do, for someone I did not like, against someone I did like. I consciously did not wish to do it and had the queerest feeling as though I were being pushed. I realized I had done similar things before. Only this time I knew I wasn't being pushed by anyone." Analysis of the situation disclosed that the patient was being forced to work toward several conflicting goals at the same time. She had been aware of something similar before but this time she felt it as an emotional experience. She felt actually pulled in different directions.

Further analysis showed up old insights in a different way as well as some new ones. Once again she saw how she was always doing whatever anyone asked her—without considering the consequences—even though she had repeatedly found how it irritated her and interfered with other things she wished to do. Each time she was

182

driven to comply by a feeling that in this way she would be approved of and make friends. This instance aroused anxiety in her by the recognition of how all her friendships were endangered, and how other entanglements occurred because of this tendency to comply.

She became aware of her inability to resist appeal to her superior judgment. In this particular instance the president had some flaws and she felt she should not associate with an inferior person. This reinforced the compulsion to comply. She felt she must be superior for in this way also she would be approved of and make friends. She recognized a feeling of satisfaction at being able to think about and discuss the president's inferiority. This helped her to feel superior but, more important, she felt a thrill at being mean to someone.

This latter realization was most significant to her. She had formerly believed herself to have been most kind and helpful, even though she felt she had been badly treated as a child. She had gradually come to suspect she was not as kind as she previously believed, but now she discovered that was quite the opposite. She said she was really a cruel person and felt relieved after the admission. She rushed in and uncovered evidences of mean hostile acts, and her pleasure at others' discomforts and failures. She re-evaluated the resentments she had harbored against her parents. These insights were followed by a short, anxious, unproductive period. She then tackled her attitudes toward her work and realized that what lay at the root of her dissatisfaction was that she did things only to prove she could do them well, and one way to prove this was to cause another person's envy. After this she was able to appreciate the part she played in what she thought of as her husband's unreasonable attitude toward her.

Progress will manifest itself in various ways. As the subjective value of a trend is reduced, its fulfillment is no longer important. When some trends cease to operate, others become unnecessary. As you get rid of compulsions, you begin to have more freedom for yourself, more interest in improving your life and consequently you bring more constructive effort into the analysis. You will feel a new quality in your relationship with the analyst. You will regard him less as a menace when you are not forced to deceive him or to use him to satisfy neurotic needs. In everyday life you will find yourself meeting old situations in new ways and being surprised that you had ever associated fear with them. You will have an awareness of being a part of the world about you. As you gradually resolve neurotic conflicts you will gain inner freedom and increasing incentive toward development. Then you will of your own accord test out a variety of values which you have not tried before. Gradually you will voluntarily discard old patterns that have hampered you, decide on new and more substantial goals, and reach convictions that will determine your eventual philosophy of life.

This brief survey of the patient's role in analysis indicates what the patient must accomplish if he is to gain the insight essential to effecting a constructive change in his character structure. In addition we have consid-

184

ered what his feelings will be as he tackles his problems. We have pointed out what his returns are for an honest, sincere effort in his own behalf. It is a particular satisfaction to have reached the stage in our psychoanalytic understanding where we are able to state plainly and simply what an individual may expect during analysis. To some of you who are contemplating analysis these considerations may cause you to feel that what lies before you is a tremendous task, that the expectations are too great, and the anticipated upheavals too frightening. It will be reassuring to know that your analyst expects to work right along with you, and to put forth his best effort to understand you and to help you reach your goal.

What Does the Analyst Do?

KAREN HORNEY, M.D.

Psychoanalytical therapy is an exquisitely co-operative enterprise. It can succeed only if both patient and analyst do their share. In the preceding chapter, how the patient contributes to the work was described. Let us now consider the various ways in which the analyst tries to help the patient.

The analyst responds to the patient's unreserved frankness with undivided attention. His attention is of a special kind. He does not merely strain to remember the exact sequence of the patient's associations or to compute the unknown quantity in the equation. He may at times make determined efforts of this kind but, if that were all, the results would be fairly barren and inconclusive. The quality of his attention must be of a more productive nature; it can be productive only if he enters into the task completely and without reservation. He responds to the patient with all his acuteness of perception, catching on spontaneously not only to the spoken words and their content but also to the emotional undertones in the associations. He listens wholeheartedly, using the knowledge he has acquired about the particular patient, drawing on his fund of experience with human beings, and letting his own emotional reactions come into play whether they be sympathy, humor, apprehensiveness, impatience, or discouragement.

While you may like the assurance that the analyst will give you his wholehearted attention, you may be disturbed by my statement regarding his emotional responses. Perhaps you feel that his mind should be as unruffled as a mirror or as a lake on a quiet summer day. But are you not asking for the impossible? If the analyst is to enter into the analytic procedure with his whole self, how can he discard his feelings—the most alive part of him? He could not possibly choke off his impatience or his discouragement without also inactivating his sympathy and blunting his sensitivity to what is going on in you.

Let us go a step further. Might not the "undesirable" emotional reactions of your analyst even have a certain value? Assume for instance that, without being in the least aware of it, you were bent on defeating your analyst. Also assume you were to proceed under so skillful a screen of zest and eagerness that for a time your analyst would fail to notice your hidden strategies, would not his feelings—more alert than his intellect—give him a signal of warning? He would detect vague feelings of irritation or discouragement in himself. If he were to suppress these, they might imperceptibly dampen his effort. But if he is aware of such reactions he will begin to wonder whether perhaps the therapeutic progress is less satisfactory than he had thought. He will first question himself: Is his ambition driving him to effect a quicker cure than is actually possible? Is he affected by vestiges of claims for omnipotence? If your analyst does discover and analyze such traces of neurotic ambition in himself, it can only be to your advantage. He will become less concerned with his own glory and will be able to devote himself the more effectively to your problems. But he will also ask himself whether there is something in your attitude that might account for his dissatisfaction; he will no longer take your eagerness to co-operate at its face value and will thus become alert to your hidden frustrating maneuvers.

Such wholehearted attention is the condition for productive analytical work—as it is for any work that is not mere mechanical routine. It is directed toward the two available sources of information: first, what the patient tells him about his relations with others both in the past and in the present, about his disturbances and difficulties, about his attitude toward himself, about his phantasies and his dreams; second, all the peculiar drives and reactions which the patient acts out inadvertently in the analytical situation itself—his expectations for an easy solution of his problems, his claims for special attention or love, his need to triumph over the analyst, his vulnerability to what he conceives as coercion or humiliation.

189

It would be difficult to say which of these two sources of information is more important. Both are indispensable. However, analysis of the attitudes appearing in the analytical situation itself has the greater therapeutic value for here the patient is confronted squarely with the irrationality of his neurotic drives. The analyst may point out, for example, his compelling need to be admired, citing as evidence data the patient has given him about his life such as his feeling easily slighted, or his surrounding himself exclusively with people who admire him. The patient may remain unconvinced, arguing that his friends are people whom he happens to like, that he simply *is* superior and that his irritation at slights is absolutely justified each time. But if he is shown that in the analytical situation, too, he is merely bent on presenting himself as a superior person and that in so doing he is actually defeating his own purpose, he can hardly escape the realization that an irrational force is operating within himself.

Accordingly these very attitudes, if overlooked or insufficiently analyzed, have the greatest power to retard the analysis and may even entirely frustrate the efforts of patient and analyst both. Such feelings may appear openly in conscious claims for love or special consideration, in undisguised anger, or in attempts to berate the analyst. They may appear in disguised form in dreams or within the train of associations.

Thus one of my patients, during a period of blockage, recalled how he had to wait in a harbor for the boat that was to carry him to an island near the shore. There was no telling when the boat would leave. It might take two, three, or four hours until the freight was stored away. In the meantime he could do nothing but sit around and wait. The memory expressed most accurately what he felt at the time in reference to the analysis. He had relegated all the work and responsibility to me; he was just a passenger waiting for me, the captain, to make a move.

The patient's attitudes may, finally, determine the spirit in which he presents his associations. Thus he may say everything that comes to his mind but in a spirit of docility, defiance, bravado, or arrogant superiority to the analyst.

You may wonder how the analyst can make sense of the jumble of the patient's free associations. He proceeds on the assumption that elements appearing in sequence are connected with each other though they may seem incoherent. Instead of going into detail * I shall only mention some important clues. The analyst constantly has in mind the question: why does this particular memory, thought, feeling, phantasy, or dream come up just now? Thus an embarrassing early experience may be recalled by the patient because he feels humiliated at having to face his present weakness. Snakes, witches, or gangsters may appear in his dreams because his own hidden aggressiveness is beginning to disquiet him. The analyst will often get the proper perspective on the meaning of associations by connecting them with the

* You will find several examples illustrating the meaning of trains of associations in Karen Horney, *Self-Analysis*, Chapter IV (W. W. Norton and Company, 1941).

subject approached by the patient in the previous analytic session.

For instance, in one session a patient may have come close to seeing exploiting tendencies in himself. In the following one he dwells on incidents in which he has been cheated. He also mentions a relative who is said to have been harmed by analysis. He considers the desirability of having a thorough physical checkup. What he is actually expressing in various versions is his fear of having to face his exploiting tendencies. As he sees it he never exploits anyone but is constantly being cheated and taken advantage of by others. He voices his concern that analysis will harm him. Here again, without being aware of it, he refers to his fear that analysis will spoil his image of himself as a good, upstanding person by exposing his exploiting tendencies. When the analyst questions his desire for a physical checkup, the patient tries to brush this aside: "Oh, I've been wanting one for a long time." "Let us see, nevertheless," the analyst insists, "why this old wish of yours emerges just now." And it may then become apparent that the idea of a medical examination, rational in itself, covers up the patient's aversion to examining himself psychologically. He is unconsciously attempting to solve his real predicament by playing around with the hope that his troubles might not be psychic at all.

A clue often lies in the recurrence in variations of one and the same theme in the course of a session. Another clue can be found in the patient's involving himself in contradictions. Changes of mood occurring in or between analytical hours point to unconscious emotional reactions to matters discussed. Sometimes a clue lies not in what the patient says but rather in what he omits. He may, for instance, dwell only on the shortcomings of others and never mention his own share in difficulties that arise. Finally, the analyst may be struck by contradictions between the patient's reports about his dealings with others and the way the patient behaves toward him. In his reports he may appear as one who is unfairly treated despite his goodness and generosity; in his behavior toward the analyst he may be berating and domineering.

I have dwelt on the quality of the analyst's attention and understanding because all the help he can give the patient follows from his understanding. Allowing for some exaggeration, analysts would need no books on analytical technique if their understanding were complete. Actually, of course, it never can be complete. Each patient confronts the analyst with problems which he has not encountered before in that specific form and combination. A line of approach that was profitable with four patients may be ineffective with the fifth. There is no blueprint to guide us. We cannot hold the patient responsible for our temporary failure to understand or to help him by ascribing it to his "resistance." Such an approach would be as futile as any shifting of responsibilities. What is needed is more and more understanding.

Assuming now that the analyst has arrived at some understanding of the patient's character, how does he utilize it toward helping the patient to understand himself and to change on the basis of the insight gained? To begin with, the analyst gives interpretations—that is, suggestions as to the possible meanings—of what the patient has expressed. The aim of interpretations is to uncover unconscious processes. They may concern the patient's unconscious compulsive needs such as his neurotic need for affection, for control, or for triumph. These processes may concern an unconscious conflict between the patient's need for independence and his equally great need to shirk responsibility. They may concern his attempts at solving conflicts by creating an idealized image of himself, by keeping at a distance from people, by resigning himself to a humble place in life, by discarding reality and living in phantasy and so forth. Unconscious processes may concern the ways in which the patient's neurotic trends, conflicts, or attempts at solution operate in his life, in the analytical situation, or in his dreams. They may concern the inner needs that compel him to cling tenaciously to his particular neurotic solutions. Most important of all, they may concern the cramping influences that all neurotic formations have on the patient's life, on his self-confidence, on his happiness, on his work, on his love life, and on his social relations. They may, finally, concern the ways in which all these factors contribute to create and maintain the patient's symptoms and manifest disturbances—the bearing they have on his phobia, his insomnia, his taking to drink, his spells of migraine, or his inhibitions about work.

Despite what you have read in preceding chapters it

194

may still strike you as incongruous that I mention, at the tail end, interpretations which provide an understanding of the manifest disturbances. You may still have the feeling that the unraveling and eventual removal of symptoms is your main reason for considering analysis. Despite better knowledge, you may still cherish the belief that if it were not for your depression or your inhibition about work you would be quite all right. But the earlier you relinquish this illusion the better it is for you. If you are organically ill it is self-evident to you that your pain, your cough, your fever *are* not your illness but are merely signs that there is some disorder in your lungs, your intestines, your joints, etc. You are also aware of the fact that the diseases to be feared most are those which, like certain forms of cancer or tuberculosis, insidiously affect bodily organs without giving you any warning signal in the form of pain or which give it only when it is too late to do anything about the disease. Exactly the same is true of your psychic disturbances. Your irritability, your fatigue, your sleeplessness *are* not the disease; they, too, are but alarm signals warning you that there is some hidden disorder in your personality. You should regard them as friends who persistently remind you that it is time to examine yourself. A young patient who was sent to me much against her will because she suffered from epileptic fits, later on almost blessed these fits because they were instrumental in making her face her conflicts and thus ultimately saved her from wasting her life.

Accordingly, try not to be impatient if your analyst

195

does not seem to be too interested at first in your street phobia or whatever plagues you, and pries instead into all sorts of things you feel are irrelevant and none of his business. Naturally you would prefer to have your phobia removed without having to go through the painful process of changing. Perhaps you will reread the chapter What Is a Neurosis? and you will understand that it cannot be done this way. You can be reasonably sure, however, that as you understand and overcome your neurotic attitudes, the phobia, too, will gradually recede. The fact that your analyst wants you to become interested in yourself and not merely in your phobia does not mean, however, that he loses sight of it. Whenever he sees a connection between your neurotic trends or conflicts and your presenting complaints, he will point it out to you and, as the analysis progresses, you will come to see such connections of your own accord.

Since a major and chronic disturbance has several roots in your personality, the analyst will have to search for all of them and present them to you as they become accessible. Let us assume, for instance, that what disturbs you most is your inhibition toward productive and creative work. At some stage of the analysis, the analyst may realize that you behave toward it as a schoolboy behaves toward an assignment he is forced to do. He will suggest that you feel it as a coercion. At first you consider this ridiculous because you really wish to write the particular paper that is causing you difficulties. But gradually you come to understand the meaning of your reluctance on this score. Although you wish to write the

196

paper, you did not anticipate the work it would entail. The ideas should simply flow from your pen. Maybe they do at the beginning. But then you actually have to formulate, to organize, to check whether you are really expressing what you want to say—in short, you have to work. And you rebel at just that. Your analyst may recognize at a later time that it is not only your neurotic version of freedom that makes you rebel but also that you feel it as an insult, as a positive humiliation that you, the mastermind, should have to do laborious work. Again, later he finds out that you are much more alert when you are with somebody who stimulates you or with whom you can argue and prove your superiority, that you get listless at the point when this exciting game of "who defeats whom" stops and you are left to your own resources. He may have arrived at this conclusion from observing you act similarly in the analytical situation.

In order to be effective, interpretations must not only be to the point but they must also be given at the proper time. An interpretation, however pertinent, may be meaningless to the patient if it is not correctly timed. Under the circumstances it would neither help nor harm. It may happen, though rarely, that a premature interpretation upsets the patient without benefiting him. A well-timed interpretation will set the patient thinking along constructive lines; it will help him to get out of blind alleys; and it will give him a better understanding of himself.

Sometimes the analyst can proceed only by trial and

error. But the more comprehensive his knowledge of the patient's character structure, the clearer he will be in his mind about the sequence in which unconscious forces should be tackled. He cannot, for instance, tackle a patient's fear of being rejected or despised or his fear of being "phony," as long as the patient visualizes himself as a saint or as a supreme lover. The analyst will avoid pointing out to the patient his need to exploit and berate others, as long as he views himself primarily as a helpless and innocent victim.

Sometimes the analyst is not in a position to offer even a tentative interpretation. He may merely feel that the whole situation somehow lacks clarity, that the patient is moving in circles, or that the specific problem under discussion is not yet satisfactorily solved. He may have all these impressions without being able to put his finger on the source of the trouble. Under these circumstances he can do no more than observe as accurately as possible and convey his impressions to the patient. This is by no means unimportant, because it helps the patient to become aware of the existing difficulty and elicits his incentive to look for the cause. It disturbs a spurious contentment with the progress of the analysis or with a particular solution and thereby calls upon untapped resources.

After making an interpretation, the analyst observes with utmost care how the patient responds to it. Sometimes the truth may strike immediately and forcefully. In such a case the patient will feel that the interpretation "clicks" and things will occur to him which confirm

198

it. New avenues of investigation will open up. In other instances the patient's associations may lead to modifications or qualifications of what has been suggested. But his readiness to accept an interpretation may also be deceptive. He may still be too eager to please the analyst. He may accept the interpretation glibly, enjoying its intellectual subtlety without in the least applying it to himself. He may also be all too glad to follow the analyst's suggestion because it diverts attention from more painful and hidden subjects.

But it is not only the question of acceptance or rejection of an interpretation that counts. All kinds of emotional reactions may ensue. For instance, the patient may merely feel that it was foolish of him to have exposed himself that much and become angry at the analyst for having found him out. He may feel unjustly accused and go on the defensive immediately, bending all his energies toward disproving the suggestion. He may feel nothing but humiliation because the analyst has pointed out a factor that contrasts with his idealized image of himself. Instead of testing out whatever truth there may be in the suggestion, he will become vindictive and try to frustrate the analyst or to humiliate him in turn. Such reactions often put the analyst's skill to a test because they are usually expressed indirectly. The patient may be entirely unaware of them. He may try to consider things rationally and become blocked because the existing unconscious feelings prevent him from being productive. If the analyst recognizes emotional reactions of this kind, he usually finds them valua-

199

ble for they help him determine along what lines he should proceed.

The ultimate aim of interpretations is to bring about changes in the patient. Such changes may be conspicuous or even dramatic. They are usually the result not only of one interpretation but of the preceding work as well. Anxiety may suddenly abate; a depression may lift; a headache may disappear. But there may be other changes, less obvious, yet no less important. The patient's attitude toward others or toward some particular person may change; he may take a different view of a neurotic factor in himself; he may become interested in a problem of which he had not previously been aware; he may begin to observe himself better and to catch on to a neurotic reaction of his own accord. You will learn more about these changes in the next chapter.

The analyst, hence, pays attention not only to the measure with which the patient accepts or rejects an interpretation, not only to the ensuing emotional reactions, but also to the kind of changes that take place. He will be particularly alert to the absence of any changes and, if none occur, he will point this out to the patient and search with him for the factors that are still interfering with the possibility of changes.

The analyst's task comprises more than the mere uncovering of unconscious processes. Integrated with and essential to the analytic process are two additional ways in which he helps the patient. One is a kind of philosophical help, an intellectual clarification of issues that are

200

important for living; the other is what I shall call a general human help.

At one time or another during his analysis, the patient will become interested in questions such as these: what are ideals and what is the value of having ideals? How do they differ from compulsive neurotic standards? What exactly does it mean to assume responsibility for oneself? What *is* inner independence? Of course many patients have thought about these questions; some may even have thought about them a great deal; others have taken them for granted; again others have discarded them as meaningless. In any case the patient will become interested in them or renew his interest when he begins to find out that, without knowing it, his thinking in this regard has been muddled. It has been confused not because he lacked intelligence but because in the matter of values he was driven in opposite directions. Thus he often confounded authentic ideals with imposed duties, self-reliance with self-accusation, self-acceptance with self-indulgence, freedom with license, love with dependency, and so on.

When the patient realizes how contradictory his attitudes on this score have been and how many unconscious pretenses he has developed in order to blind himself to the existence of these contradictions, he begins to struggle for intellectual clarity. The analyst, then, will help the patient to clarify his goals in life. He will say in essence: "You speak in glowing terms of independence. Fine! but merely doing as you please, being cynical or unconventional does not make you independent. True independence entails being resourceful, assuming responsibilities, living by your convictions. Of course it is up to you to decide whether you really want independence. But if you do, you will have to examine and eventually overcome all those factors within yourself which interfere with this goal such as expecting too much of others, putting the blame on others, and so forth."

Such a discussion of values differs from the reading of books or from a talk with a friend in that it is combined with a scrutiny of the personal emotional problems involved.

When I speak of general human help I mean the way the analyst helps the patient—not through his interpretations but through his attitude toward the patient. This includes his willingness to understand, his unflagging interest in the patient's growth, his faith in the patient's existing potentialities, his firmness that permits him to view the patient's suffering with concern without letting himself be crushed by them, to remain unswayed by the patient's admiration and undaunted by the patient's aggressive demands or hostile attacks. The value of such an attitude is underrated by some and overrated by others. Freud understood the task of the analyst as primarily an intellectual one. The less the analyst's personality was involved, the more effective the therapy would be. The advice he gave on this score was in negative terms: the analyst should *not* be condemnatory; the analyst should *not* yield to the patient's neurotic demands. At the other extreme are some modern analysts

202

who contend that the very friendship the analyst extends to the patient is essential in curing him of his disturbances in human relationships. Such notions, while flattering to the analyst and pleasing to the patient, may easily blur the fundamental issue, namely that patient and analyst come together in order to do work.

You may wonder at this point whether the relationship between patient and analyst is not a kind of friendship. In a sense, it is friendship at its very best but I always hesitate to regard it as such because it does, after all, lack the measure of spontaneity and mutuality essential to real friendship. The question was clarified for me by the distinction John Macmurray makes between personal and functional relationships:

This is the characteristic of personal relationships. They have no ulterior motive. . . . They do not serve partial and limited ends. . . . Friendship, fellowship, communion, love are all in one way or another liable to convey a false or partial meaning. But what is common to them all is the idea of a relationship between us which has no purpose beyond itself; in which we associate because it is natural for human beings to share their experience, to understand one another, to find joy and satisfaction in living together; in expressing and revealing themselves to one another.†

According to Macmurray, all relationships that have a purpose over and beyond personal friendship are functional. Thus, when you join others in a scientific or political group your association with them is determined

† John Macmurray, *Reason and Emotion*. D. Appleton–Century Company, New York, 1938.

by the purpose of discussing scientific or political matters. In this sense the relationship between patient and
analyst is essentially a functional one. Your analyst and
you may mutually like and respect each other. Yet you
enter into the relationship for a definite purpose: to free
you from your neurotic shackles and thereby create better conditions for your future growth as a human being.
This definition is also satisfactory in that it leaves the
emphasis where it should be, namely on the work to
be done.

It remains true, however, that the human help which
the analyst gives the patient is important and even indispensable within the framework of the analytic process.
I am thinking here primarily of the analyst's consistent
emphasis on what he believes to be the patient's best
interests. In principle this is the attitude every good
physician has toward his patient. But the difference lies
in that the analyst's task is infinitely more comprehensive. The surgeon's job is usually circumscribed. The
analyst's work on the other hand involves no less than
the patient's whole future development as a human being. The questions he has in mind regarding his patient
are somewhat comparable to the questions raised by a
good educator: what furthers or hinders his development into a good, constructive human being? How can
he best develop his potentialities, whether these be special talents or such general qualities as strength, courage,
considerateness, or kindness?

You may feel unpleasantly reminded here of the
"mother knows best what is good for you" attitude.

There are, however, significant differences between the mother-child situation and that in analysis. The patient is no longer a child but is able to evaluate by himself where his best interest lies when he is helped to see the issues clearly. Moreover, the analyst is not authoritative but endeavors to find out together with the patient in what manner he is blocking his own way.

It is the analyst's consistent focus on the patient's best interest that eventually helps him to gain the latter's confidence. Of course, the patient would never have decided to work with the analyst if he had not had some confidence in him to begin with. But his initial confidence, though based on a good intuitive feeling, is not built on especially solid ground. After all, most of us are aware of the difference between an intuitive trusting of another person and the repeated, concrete evidence of his reliability. For the neurotic, however, this difference is considerably greater. With all his anxieties, suspicions, and defensive hostilities—conscious or unconscious—he needs proof after proof before he can dare take the risk of really trusting someone.

As for the analyst's nonauthoritative attitude, I prefer to define it in positive terms as an endeavor to place the patient under his own jurisdiction. The analyst firmly believes in the desirability of every person taking his life into his own hands, as far as possible, and assuming responsibility for himself. He respects individual differences and knows that each person can ultimately decide only in accordance with his own wishes and his own ideals. Hence he sees his main task as helping the

205

patient to recognize his own wishes and find his own set of values.

This attitude is responsible to a large degree for the analyst's reluctance to give advice. Another perfectly good and simple reason for his reluctance on this score is that in most cases he feels incapable of giving advice. Being more aware of the complexities of the human mind than most people, he has developed an attitude of realistic humility that allows him to be fully aware of his own limitations. Naturally he will express his opinion whenever it is clear to him that the patient is about to act against his own interest. Furthermore, if certain of the patient's symptoms point to the possibility of an organic disorder, he will suggest a physical examination. He may definitely advise against a major decision if he is convinced that the patient is acting under the pressure of irrational emotional factors.

Although you will agree that such an attitude on the part of the analyst is helpful in making you more independent, you may not always like it. You may want guidance. You may expect at the beginning that the analyst will solve all your problems by making a decision for you. You may insist that he has answers for everything, but is withholding them for some mysterious reason. Try to remember, then, that he can often be more helpful to you by trying to understand the background of your question or indecision.

Another way in which the analyst helps the patient is his attitude of accepting him as he is. What does this mean and why is it important? It may mean scientific objectivity. Freud expected the analyst to look at the patient with the eyes of a scientist and to eliminate value judgments. This, however, necessarily creates an artificial situation because no one can exclude his set of values when human behavior and motivations are involved. Actually, the patient himself does not believe in such objectivity but assumes that it is adopted for the sake of therapy.

It may mean tolerance. Tolerance is, of course, important in view of the self-condemning attitude harbored by most patients. Although the patient may distrust this attitude, too, it is actually genuine by virtue of the analyst's understanding.

It means, finally, that the analyst is interested in the patient as a human being who is engaged in the process of development and that he appreciates the patient's every move ahead. In order to help you to understand the value of such an attitude I must tell you something that may surprise you. When he begins analysis, the patient as a rule is not interested in himself as he *is*. He is constantly concerned with what he *should* be and blames himself for his shortcomings instead of tackling them realistically. Naturally this has to be analyzed. But it is also the analyst's consistent interest in him as he is and as he could be that helps the patient to develop a constructive interest in his real self.

The analyst can have this positive attitude because he believes in the constructive forces within the patient which will eventually enable him to resolve his neurotic conflicts. Is this a blind optimism on the part of the

207

analyst, or is it a realistic faith in the existence of such forces or at least in existing potentialities? On the basis of our experience it is a most realistic faith. Initially, the patient's constructive, forward-moving forces may lie buried under illusions, hopelessness, *and* destructiveness. But with rare exceptions we see them come to life during analysis.

As he gains insight into the workings of his mind, the patient gradually comes to feel: "*I* can do something; *I* can have feelings other than mere irritation and fear; *I* can like somebody; *I* can enjoy things. *I* can want." And with each taste of freedom and of strength his incentive to gain more of it grows. The analyst's belief in and clear recognition of the patient's potentialities helps the patient to regain his faith in himself. This is particularly important at those periods in analysis when the patient loses faith in himself or when it dawns upon him how little of it he has ever had.

The analyst thus takes a most active part in the analytical process. He observes and examines the patient's every move, the flow of his associations, his reactions to interpretations, the variety of ever-changing attitudes toward the analyst and toward the analytical situation, the changes that take place in his relations to others and toward himself and in his set of values. But the analyst does not merely follow the patient. Through his interpretations, explanations, and questions, he influences the course of the analysis. He helps the patient out of blind

208

alleys and suggests scrutiny along more profitable lines. He encourages the patient to persist in working at a problem even though he is caught in the clutches of some emotional reaction. By means of these activities the analyst actually conducts the analysis. And this is as it should be. For while analysis is a co-operative enterprise between patient and analyst, it is the analyst who for many reasons carries the greater responsibility.

How Does Analysis Help?

MURIEL IVIMEY, M.D.

OUR EXPERIENCE shows that many people who are interested in psychoanalysis and believe in its therapeutic value have no clear idea of exactly how it helps, what the results are, and how results come about. "Is it sufficient for a person to become aware of his neurotic trends and conflicts?" is a question that is frequently brought up in discussions. No, it is not enough. In addition to becoming aware of his neurotic trends, a person needs to become aware of their purposes and aims, the forces involved, and the interrelations, interreactions, and repercussions of neurotic elements and forces. He also needs to discover the constructive forces within himself which make it possible for him to bring about necessary changes. Awareness of the existence of neurotic trends is only the first step toward extricating oneself from neurotic patterns of living. Another question frequently raised is: "When you know what is wrong with you, what do you do?" This question will be answered in this chapter. The ultimate goal in analytic treatment is to bring about changes in the personality which enable the individual to dispense with neurotic trends, to resolve inner conflicts, to find and develop his real self, his real values and goals, and to start on a new way of life.

Neurosis and the disturbances and complaints that bring the individual to analysis are the consequences of unresolved inner conflicts. While he has made various attempts to solve his inner conflicts, he has not really succeeded. He cannot resolve them realistically and incisively as long as basic anxiety—that is, feelings of helplessness, isolation, and hostility—lies in the depths of his personality. For these feelings force him to persist in all his irreconcilable compulsive ways. In order that conflicts may be truly resolved, the internal conditions—helplessness, isolation, and hostility—must change. In the process of analysis these conditions do change and basic anxiety diminishes. The patient discovers that he can do something for himself, that he does get into better and more realistic rapport with others, and that he becomes less hostile. This is brought about through analysis of neurotic elements in the personality, leading to the formulation of problems for the patient's consideration. When he finds that it is possible to tackle a problem and to effect a change in his ways, his basic anxiety is reduced simultaneously. As basic anxiety lessens progressively, the patient becomes stronger within himself, less isolated and less hostile, and his capacity to overcome compulsions increases proportionately. He can gradually dispense with the neurotic ways which have been the components of inner conflict. Thus, little by little, inner conflict is resolved.

What is really meant by analysis of neurotic tendencies? It means the thorough investigation of all elements in the highly complex structure of neurosis, one by one, collecting and organizing evidence and seeing the extent to which they ramify throughout one's life. Analysis reveals the overpowering grip they have on you; how indiscriminate and inappropriate your neurotic impulses are; how upset, desperate, anxious or panicky you become when you are blocked or frustrated in satisfying neurotic needs. Analysis helps you to discover how you have been attributing distorted and exaggerated values to your neurotic ways and that you have not established true values positively and realistically. It also helps you to see the connection between your neurotic ways and their consequences—how they affect your feeling about yourself, how they affect your relationships with others, and how they have influenced the course of your life and will continue to influence it along the same lines if you persist in them. All these data, organized clearly and concretely, shape up as a problem.

This comprehensive analysis of neurotic elements helps the patient to see his position so clearly, logically, and with such emotional conviction that there is no escaping the conclusion that something has to be done. Each neurotic trait is analyzed according to these steps and in the same detail, so that the process as a whole consists of the formulation of many specific problems in

213

sequence. The total, massive problem of the neurosis as a whole is broken down into parts which can be dealt with bit by bit.

So far, analysis has helped in clarifying problems. As each difficulty is formulated in these terms, the patient's rational judgment can come into play. When rational judgment is available, the question arises: can he do something to change? This is a turning point. In our experience, constructive forces which lie latent and untapped now make themselves felt. The patient finds himself able for the first time to do something that is different from his accustomed automatic, compulsive behavior—to act according to rational and realistic considerations rather than according to the dictates of neurotic needs.

Let us give you an example of the analysis of neurotic trends belonging to one of the main categories. This piece of analysis is not in any sense complete but it will serve to suggest what is involved and what the patient experiences. An intelligent woman of forty-five in analysis was beginning to become aware of her tendencies to comply and yield to the wishes of others, of needing to be liked, to be agreeable, to keep the peace, to do things for others, to save them trouble, and to keep her own interests and rights in the background. It was suggested that she pause and consider these tendencies in detail.

Many examples were found, and evidence piled up from different periods of her life. As a young girl she had always been the one to step into the breach and take over in emergencies, until she took it to be the accepted

214

thing even under ordinary circumstances and so did those about her. She did not go to college because she did not want to make an issue of her interests and wishes. She married her suitor because he pleaded so persistently, although she was not in love with him. She thought love would come later. Although she was miserably unhappy, she did not want to "make trouble" by bringing matters to open discussion with her husband. She decided on divorce and it went through. She then settled down to devoting her life to her son, repeating the same pattern. It was an agonizing thought to her that there was no love and understanding between herself and her son. He became extremely dependent on her, egocentric and defiant; otherwise, by and large, he shut her out of his life.

As the patient's more recent life and present day-by-day events were explored, it appeared that the same trends were also present in her relationships with other members of the family, with men she had met since the divorce, in social affairs, and with people in her job situation, in casual encounters with people as she went about the city, in buses, taxis, and shops, and when she went on vacations. Under all circumstances she was agreeable, overmodest, yielding, and appeasing. Certain sensitivities came to light. She was uncomfortable whenever disagreements arose or when anything approaching an argument or a fight appeared imminent. She was sensitive to displeasure or anger in others; if someone failed to greet her cordially, she would fear he had taken a dislike to her.

215

She was unable to stand up for herself. Not only was she too forebearing with her son and with one or two egocentric and aggressive members of her family but she sometimes submitted to real injustice. Recently an old friend had accused her of something she did not do. She let the matter go by. She thought to herself that her friend was always doing that kind of thing, especially to her; the friend was high-strung and irresponsible; she was neurotic and had problems of her own. The patient thought it would cause trouble if the matter were challenged. Perhaps it would disrupt their friendship, and this she could not stand. She felt the same way about her son; he had problems and, if she made an issue of anything, it would disturb their relationship. Following the incident with her friend, she felt upset and depressed; later she developed a splitting headache and did not sleep that night.

Further discussion revealed how relentless these impulses were. The patient began to see that rather than following a natural inclination, as she was used to thinking of it, she was compulsively driven to behave in the same way with all people and under all circumstances, and that she could not act otherwise. The more she considered it, the more clearly she realized that she was in the grip of powerful forces that controlled her.

Analysis then focused on another aspect of these tendencies—that is, her subjective values for them. She was firmly convinced that she was perfectly right, that her behavior was necessary and desirable, and that it showed fine, high-minded qualities. "I am only being a

216

good mother, a good sister, a good friend, a responsible member of society. . . . This world would be a better place if people were more considerate." As a matter of fact, she said, if everyone looked out for himself, everybody would be fighting everybody else. It would be dog eat dog. It would be indecent and immoral if she behaved differently than she did.

Other aspects of her compliancy trends were brought to light. She was out for the satisfaction of needs to sacrifice her own interests for those of others. But what were the actual results in her relationships with others and how had her behavior affected the course of her life? It appeared that the balance was far over on the debit side. She took some satisfaction in the fact that certain people turned to her in trouble and asked her advice but she took no pleasure in helping them and had no feeling of warmth, closeness, or sympathy. She commented on how people took her for granted, how little they thought of her and her needs. It was pointed out that this might be the result of her not letting her interests and needs be known. An especially painful part of this phase of analysis was the consideration of the effect her compliant and self-effacing behavior had upon her relationship with her son. It was painful because the compliant and self-sacrificing qualities she cherished so highly were part of her idealized image of herself which was analyzed somewhat later. For the time being the focus was kept on the connection between these trends and her son's dependency and his demands on her.

The situation with her friend was considered in more

detail. The patient had said nothing when she was accused unjustly. The incident served as evidence of a rather severe inhibition in standing up for herself. While it was being turned over and considered from various angles, many questions arose. What was she hoping to gain by letting herself be stepped on? She expected appreciation and loyalty. What did she get? Did she really like this alleged friend? Was she motivated by genuine consideration for her friend and by understanding forebearance or was she forced by her own inner compulsive needs to cling to the relationship? Was she not paying a high price for this relationship, in headaches and sleeplessness, in humiliation and in letting herself be the butt of hostile remarks?

Analysis clarified the nature of these trends, their aims, their ramifications throughout her life, their indiscriminateness, their compulsiveness, the values she had for them and their consequences. These factors, so organized, presented a problem. The patient began to get interested in herself; there was some relief in having something definite concerning her difficulties to think about. She began to reconsider and revaluate. While she was in the process of doing this, she met her old friend. They had luncheon together, in the course of which the friend came out with a caustic and unjustifiably critical remark. The patient had been thinking about the relationship; she had been seeing herself and her friend in a new light. To her surprise, she rose to the occasion and refuted the statement in no uncertain terms. The friend was taken aback and made a lame apology.

In recounting the incident in a subsequent analytic session, the patient said she felt wonderful. True, she had trembled all over, her heart had beat fast, and she had been sarcastic and self-righteous. These observations were put to one side for the time being. As a result of this change in behavior, the patient felt for the first time that she could do something about herself. This meant the beginning of changes in internal conditions which had hitherto forced her to adhere to her neurotic compliant pattern. She felt less helpless, less dominated by her compulsive appeasing tendencies, less enslaved in her relationship with her friend, and she was encouraged at having taken a step toward standing up for herself. She felt less in awe of her friend and more natural although she said there was something about her own behavior that was not yet quite right. However, she felt that there was a better understanding in as far as she had come out with her real feeling. She felt less lonely, somewhat stronger, and more self-respecting. She said: "I guess I'm not such a lovely character—think of me fighting!"

She started to work at her compliancy trends seriously and with determination. In the course of time the automaticity of her conciliatory, submissive impulses lessened. She came to be sincere, direct, and effective in her helpfulness and willing to confide in reliable friends when she was in difficulties.

Next, tendencies of a different nature were taken up for consideration. In the course of our discussion of compliancy trends, aggressive tendencies were noted from

219

time to time. Focusing on these brought up many instances of needs to direct and control others, to make excessive demands, to insist on being first, to be suspicious of ulterior motives in others that might put her at a disadvantage. Although these needs and expressions of them had been in the main rigidly repressed, they had nevertheless been felt whenever she was prevented from getting the upper hand. They had been expressed quite openly in close relationships, as with her former husband and her son. In the latter case she had rationalized aggressive tendencies as perfectly natural and laudable maternal concern for his welfare and development.

Frequent resentment and spells of rage, which she tried to control, stemmed from frustration when others opposed her. In addition, the repression of aggressive trends forced her to dam back even legitimate, self-assertive impulses lest she reveal any vestige of self-interest. This resulted in submission to others in quite self-abasing ways. She was enraged at those whom she permitted to exploit her and triumph over her and at herself for being weak and spineless. These hostile impulses had two-fold repercussions: they enhanced her fears of the hostility of others toward her, and they tended to lower her self-esteem and thus added to her self-recriminations and to her feelings of inner weakness.

Aggressive trends were analyzed along the same lines and in the same detail as were compliancy trends. By this process they took shape as problems which came within range of the patient's capacity to judge and reconsider. When they were seen in a new light, her interest in tackling the problems they represented was aroused and she found she could cope with one situation, then with another, in rational and appropriate ways. She felt further improvement in inner strength, better rapport with others, and less hostility. Her relationships with others became better; she was less prone to dictate to them and manage their lives. She became less suspicious and could appreciate the rights of others and their positive qualities. She saw her own part in situations in which others reacted with tension, resentment, and counterattack. She began to see that much of her so-called helpfulness actually constituted an attempt to dominate and that much of the lack of appreciation she encountered was not unjustified. She saw also that the very manner of her yielding to others was often actually designed to put them in the wrong and to make them suffer the consequences.

Tendencies to withdraw, to avoid emotional involvement with others, quite marked in this patient, were analyzed much later. They were deeply buried but work on trends of the other two categories cleared the way for their emergence. Withdrawal trends were manifested in being cold and distant; in preserving her independence to an extreme degree; in attempting to be self-sufficient in order not to be under obligations; and in generally avoiding any closeness to others. These tendencies were clarified and brought within range of the patient's comprehension and ability to make changes. When she understood her aims, the enhanced values she had for them and their consequences, she was able gradually to come

221

closer to people, to experience her own emotional reactions, to be responsive to the feelings of others. Her excessive independence and self-sufficiency loosened up. She continued to work at these tendencies with the result that her loneliness disappeared; she felt herself becoming a part of the life around her.

Analysis of and work on trends that we have discussed so far does not actually proceed in a strictly methodical way nor do the results occur in as orderly and satisfying a fashion as is suggested. One short paragraph in this chapter covers weeks and sometimes months of work on one group of trends, rarely steady and uninterrupted. Material comes up that necessitates turning aside from the topic at hand for a few sessions or for a longer period. However, as consistently as possible, but with no rigid insistence, analysis concentrates on one problem at a time. Results are achieved and inner changes are felt little by little. As a rule, astounding revelations and dazzling bursts of insight do not take place. There are times when something becomes very clear and the patient feels a great sense of relief and finds he can do something that had formerly been impossible. This occurs from time to time in the process as a whole and should be taken in context with the whole job of analysis of a very complex structure. Changes are gradual, including the moments of greater clarification and release. Improvement is slow.

In the course of discussions, many contradictions and inconsistencies came to light and, from time to time, the patient's attention was called to them. Frequently she regarded them blandly and casually, showing that she felt there was nothing unusual about them; at times she showed irritation or anxiety. These observations led to scrutiny of the ways in which she managed to avoid seeing discrepancies in her personality and to consideration of what defenses were endangered when she became irritated or anxious.

The patient had developed an idealized image of herself of phantastic proportions. To put it briefly, she thought of herself as being perfectly considerate, gentle, and long-suffering (compliancy trends); all wise and foreseeing in guiding others (directing and controlling trends); and entirely objective and immune to feelings which would obscure her sense of duty and her best judgment (withdrawing trends). Analysis of this idealized image was partly accomplished little by little while her enhanced and distorted values for the qualities associated with each neurotic trend were investigated. As work on the trends proceeded, she came to see how her glamorized version of herself had prevented her from recognizing discrepancies in her personality. Another consequence of her self-idealization was that in her compulsive allegiance to this goddesslike image, she unconsciously regarded herself as beneath contempt and utterly worthless. She derogated her real abilities; she loathed and despised her real weaknesses and failings. It was understandable that she never could face them, much less begin to free herself of them as long as she entertained high-flown illusions about herself. Still another consequence of her self-idealization was that she held herself in a strait jacket of self-imposed demands and she actually tried to live up to her own impossible dictates. Since she was subject to human weaknesses, she was constantly disgusted and enraged at herself.

In the course of time, she came to understand more clearly the significance of her self-aggrandizement, her arrogance, and her complete lack of a realistic estimate of her positive qualities and potentialities as well as of her faults. Work on this problem brought her to a sounder footing with herself; she was able to dispel her illusions, to accept herself, and to work realistically toward becoming a better human being. This made still further inroads on her basic anxiety. As a perfect person, there would be no reason why she should become stronger whereas, as a fallible human being not omnipotent but with real abilities, she could strive to lift herself out of her state of helplessness and to become stronger. As a perfect human being, she would have very little in common with ordinary people and would thus perpetuate her isolation from them whereas, as an ordinary mortal, she could feel closer to others and more tolerant of their shortcomings, while striving at the same time to improve herself and to help others. As a superwoman, she would be constantly offended by the lack of deference she felt entitled to whereas, when she brought herself down to earth, these exorbitant claims evaporated and she could appreciate the regard she did receive. Her relationships with others improved and so did her relationship with herself.

224

The patient's tendencies to externalize her difficulties were manifest in her preoccupation with other people's problems. In this way she could avoid awareness of her own inner problems, her neurotic ways, and her contradictions and inconsistencies. Analysis of these tendencies clarified her compulsive concern about helping others and directing them in the way they should go. It showed her how this way of blinding herself to inner conflicts reinforced her needs to do things for others (compliancy trends) and to manage their lives (aggressive trends). It showed her that frequently the qualities and faults and motivations, which she was so convinced existed in others, did not actually exist in them but were the reflection of parts of herself. She saw how ineffectual she was, for her absorption in other people's problems amounted in large part to ruminations only, in some part to "fussing" about minor practical issues, and in general contained no element of genuine, active, and constructive interest in essentials.

Not only did her tendency to externalize blind her to her own problems but she tended to demand that others change their attitudes toward her and their treatment of her as a cure for her unhappiness. This was manifested particularly in her insistent focus on her son's problems; if he would only change toward her, her own problems would be solved. An interesting by-product of analysis of her tendencies to externalize was her understanding of one of her symptoms, one which she had taken for a minor, innocent eccentricity. This was her compulsive neatness. She was exquisitely sensitive to any sort of external disorder and was always compulsively tidying up and straightening out things about her. Further light was thrown on this behavior in the detailed analysis of other elements in her personality. When externalizing tendencies were seen as a defense against facing and coming to grips with real difficulties in herself, she was able to turn her attention inward and make more progress toward solution of her own problems.

Other major defenses against awareness of inner conflicts were analyzed in turn. She had been blinding herself to discrepancies by convincing herself that her tendencies to sacrifice herself and to yield to others constituted her main, or only, characteristics. She saw why she had had to attempt to wipe out aggressive impulses or force them into the background, why she was so exaggeratedly conciliatory and appeasing: the discrepancies were so great that she did not dare allow herself to experience them. It was impossible to reconcile them by any means so she had arbitrarily to convince herself that one side of the conflict did not exist. Identification and analysis of aggressive trends, as well as compliancy trends, started her working toward the reduction of each one of these irreconcilable elements. She had also utilized the device of detaching herself from inner feelings of any kind in order to avoid awareness of conflicting compulsive drives. While working on her withdrawal tendencies she saw how they had also served to blind her to contradictions in her personality. She was now able not only to come closer to people, but also to know

226

her own feelings and to become aware of contradictions in herself.

Throughout analysis subsidiary devices by which the patient managed to blur and befog issues relating to contradictory elements in her personality were picked up. She was strongly addicted to claiming arbitrary rightness for practically all her opinions and every position she held. She would take contradictory stands on one issue and stick quite tenaciously to both of her positions. For instance, she was just as positive that the younger generation is inconsiderate, cynical, arrogant, and irreverent *and* that the right attitude toward younger people is to let them decide everything for themselves, to leave them untrammeled by the experience or prejudices of former generations and free of obligations and responsibilities toward older people. Since she felt she was absolutely right in both these opinions, it was impossible for her to distinguish between her hostile attitudes and her conciliatory and self-effacing approach.

Another device she used to avoid awareness of contradictions in her feelings and impulses was to keep them all under rigid control by sheer will power. There were many examples of damming back intense feelings— longings for companionship and intimacy with others, anger, impulses to take charge and push others out of her way, and the fears, panics and psychic pain she frequently suffered. She bottled up such feelings and attempted to preserve a stoical calm. However, she suffered considerable strain and profound fatigue, partly due to the effort such control required. She would occa-

227

sionally reach the breaking point, when she would hide in her room and give way to uncontrolled emotional outbursts which seemed to come from nowhere.

Other defenses included much ingenious rationalizing. She was very prone to evade attempts to clarify issues by cleverly slipping away from a subject. One technique was to disappear behind a cloud of generalities and to reappear unexpectedly with a totally different topic. Another was to shift subtlely from one guise to another—from the guise of the martyred innocent to that of the philosophical idealist to that of the practical manager and family executive. She would resort to this sort of thing, for instance, when the discussion touched on the consequences of her compliancy trends. In discussing her values, concerning which she was so positive, she took refuge, surprisingly, in a general cynicism. In this way she attempted to dismiss all consideration of her moral values and goals in life and to avoid the necessity of making any revision.

Work on these defenses helped her to straighten out her thinking processes, clarify issues, see the real point of some difficulty and get on with further changes in her personality. As she gradually dispensed with these defenses, feelings of inner strength increased. She became less dependent on false reasoning, evasions, and rigid opinionatedness, and hence could be more direct, more flexible, more honest and courageous, more confident in herself. The tensions precipitated by excessive control of her feelings eased up and she was able to be herself without fear of uncontrollable emotional outbursts. As her cynical attitudes loosened, she was able to be definite as to what she believed was valid and valuable in life and what was not, and as to what kind of person she really wanted to be.

Throughout analysis deep-seated hopelessness and despair gave way imperceptibly, but nonetheless surely, with each bit of work successfully accomplished. She became progressively stronger inwardly and more straightforward and realistic in her dealings with people and in her handling of external situations. The feeling of being inextricably caught in insoluble conflicts was gradually dissipated and her wry and somewhat bitter attitude toward others who were enjoying life softened.

I have discussed briefly how this patient began to change. I have taken the case of one individual as an example of how work in analysis is done, what results occur, and how they occur. As far as the method is concerned, this holds true in general for the analysis of any neurotic personality, according to our present practice and experience. But each individual presents his own particular problems and special difficulties. Certain aspects of neurotic development are more strongly emphasized and more highly elaborated in one individual than in another. There is a wide margin for modifications in procedure; flexibility and ingenuity are exercised according to these special factors in the individual patient. Nevertheless, the tasks for which the analyst is responsible and those for which the patient is responsible remain the same.

The main objectives during analysis are that the pa-

tient establishes himself on a firm basis of awareness of
and confidence in his own inner capacity to do something
about himself, that he loses the sense of isolation and
estrangement from other people and instead feels himself to be on common ground with them as a human being, and finally that his blind, diffuse, and terrifying
hostility disappears. In addition, within the period of
analysis his relationships with others will become more
natural and discriminating and he will be guided by rational considerations and freer emotional response. He
can form warm, friendly and intimate relationships; he
can take care of himself in the presence of real danger
and hostile attack from others; and he will be able to
experience himself apart from others and to cultivate his
individual interests and gifts independently.

Generally speaking, analysis helps him to see that his
values were dictated by neurotic considerations and that
they were essentially inappropriate and inconsistent
with his true interests and his dignity as a human being,
that his ideals were mainly empty abstractions rather
than ideals which he really believed in and strove to
attain. By discarding false values and spurious goals he
finds real values and ideals and goals to serve as guiding
principles for his development and growth and for the
future direction of his life.

I have said something about the forces involved in
neurotic development. Let us look at analytic treatment
as a whole and at the process of change in the personality from the angle of the forces in operation in the
patient. One set of forces compels the patient to main-

tain his neurotic structure as a whole and in all its parts. In analysis these forces operate in reactionary ways and retard progress. They are expressed in the patient's fighting with every ounce of energy to maintain the status quo. His capacity for rational judgment and constructive efforts are practically unavailable. The discovery and mobilization of constructive forces in the patient is the crux of psychoanalytic therapy.

At the beginning of treatment, the balance of power is on the side of retarding forces, while the constructive forces have little or no influence. Nevertheless, they exist, as witness the patient's decision to consult the physician and undertake analysis. Positive efforts are sustained to the extent of attending analytic sessions regularly and producing material, although a patient may sometimes feel that even this is too arduous and questionable in value. On the whole, forces compelling the maintenance of the status quo dominate the situation. The patient's hopelessness is likely to add to the handicap, since it robs him of incentive and tempts him to be lackadaisical and inert.

It has been customary to refer to expressions of retarding forces as resistance to analysis on the part of the patient. Nowadays we focus on the play of inner forces of both kinds, the obstructive as well as the constructive forces. When we do this, we get a better understanding of problems of so-called resistance. In the analysis of any neurotic element in the personality, many defenses, justifications, evasions, etc. come into play. Transference reactions are also factors of very great importance in the patient's maintaining the status quo. These factors all point to a tenacious prejudice to remain as he is. He is stubborn and argumentative, ingratiating and appealing, sly, or totally noncommittal—anything to hold his own against change. We regard this not essentially as opposition or resistance to therapy, although this is the effect. The patient desperately wants to get help. But he must cling to his established ways because he has nothing else.

If this is understood, if this understanding is conveyed to the patient, and if all other aspects of neurotic elements are thoroughly analyzed, especially transference reactions, the patient comes to a more realistic view of his position. He applies himself to the task of reconsideration and revaluation and finds that there are possibilities of coping with life in other ways. He finds that he has other resources besides his neurotic devices. He finds that he can exercise rational choice as to how he will behave and what he will do and that he can act upon his choice. Analysis of so-called resistance is thus effective in helping the patient to explore his potentialities for constructive efforts, with which he will be able to overcome obstructive, retarding forces that have hitherto had the greater power over him. Constructive forces gradually gain the ascendancy. The patient can then direct his energies actively and effectively—along with the analyst's efforts in his behalf—toward constructive goals.

In our experience, as in the experience of physicians in other fields of medicine, the patient's natural, healthy resources are available to the extent to which it is possible for them to operate. Even though these resources have been overwhelmed by too powerful forces of disease processes, they are nevertheless ready to be mobilized while there is still life, provided that the physician is able to assist in shifting the balance of power. The constructive forces we count on in psychoanalysis exist in all human beings, although many are not aware of them. They are felt as impulses to be a whole person, to live fully, to be free and effective. They operate in the neurotic individual's struggles to make himself whole by means of his pseudo solutions of conflict, but he suffers too many disadvantages as a result of this crude patchwork with its multitudinous secondary bolstering mechanisms. He remains fundamentally shaky and insecure. Analysis guides the neurotic person toward undoing the elaborate patchwork and becoming strong from the ground up. His impulses to be whole are implemented by rationality, will power, determination, and by the capacity to judge intellectually and morally and to make efforts to fulfill his real wishes. Analysis affords the patient the opportunity and provides the experience of becoming a whole and soundly integrated person.

How Do You Progress After Analysis?

KAREN HORNEY, M.D.

THE VERY suggestion that you might still have problems to cope with after your analysis is terminated may arouse protest. Many of my patients were upset when I pointed out to them that they would have to continue working with themselves. They had expected to emerge from analysis as "finished products." Theirs would be a paradise of untroubled serenity where problems and conflicts did not exist and where the power to create and enjoy was absolute.

Such expectations are illusory. It is true that analysis is a means toward outgrowing your personality difficulties and developing your potentialities. And when we speak of potentialities we have in mind not only your innate talents or gifts but even more your latent power to become more direct, more wholehearted, more alive, and more effective in your human relationships and in your work. Your growth as a human being, however, is

235

a process that can and should go on as long as you live. Hence analysis as a means of gaining self-knowledge is intrinsically an interminable process. Analytical therapy, while it helps you to disentangle yourself from the web of conflicts and to develop on a sounder basis, only initiates this development; it does not and cannot complete it.

This raises a difficult question. If our growth as human beings is interminable, and if analytical therapy merely sets this process in motion, when does the patient reach the stage where he no longer needs treatment?

Originally, when Freud made his first discoveries concerning the unconscious factors that cause neuroses, this question was easily answered. The treatment was terminated when the symptom, on behalf of which the patient had sought help, had disappeared. This delightfully neat solution has proved to be fallacious. Even though the "symptom," for instance hysterical paralysis of an arm, is removed, the person remains hysterical in his way of dealing with life. Furthermore, a subsequent upset may cause the development of another symptom such as hysterical blindness.

Since psychotherapy as it has now developed deals with personality structure as a whole, it is more difficult to decide when treatment should be terminated. Our question would be: has the patient's personality improved to the extent that he can safely be dismissed from treatment?

We have tried in discussions to formulate basic criteria for such an improvement. Briefly, we arrived at formulations like these: before terminating an analysis the patient should become less rigid, less vulnerable, less arrogant, more assertive, more warmhearted, more co-operative, more honest, more realistic. Such improvements, however, while undoubtedly desirable are too relative to serve as the sole criteria. A patient's grandiose notions about himself may have diminished considerably in the course of the analysis but certain areas in his life may still be governed by wishful thinking rather than by realistic considerations. It would be difficult therefore to say exactly how realistic he should be before terminating his treatment.

Moreover, if we were to release our patient solely on the basis of what has been accomplished in the way of personality improvements, this might entail a certain danger for there would always remain some unsolved problem, some fears that could be diminished, some sensitivities that could be lessened, some inhibitions that are still disturbing. Thus if both patient and analyst focused their attention entirely on what remained to be done, they would be tempted to go on and on forever.

These criteria must be complemented, therefore, by another consideration: at what stage of his development is the patient ready to continue on his own? Of course, only those analysts will raise this question who trust that it is possible for a patient to proceed on his own, and who have relinquished the belief that the patient cannot overcome his difficulties without the analyst's help. Hence the broad question of termination becomes more precise: when can the patient deal constructively with his own problems? What capacities must he have acquired to be able to do so?

To begin with, he must have clarified his *goals* in life and he must have a clear recognition of his own values. It is not necessary or even feasible that he *attain* his goals during analysis—he can never do more than approximate them—but he must know in what direction he wants to develop. As long as he is still driven compulsively toward some goal which he considers the solution to all his neurotic problems, he cannot proceed by himself, for he will be interested merely in analyzing the factors which prevent him from attaining his particular neurotic goal. He will certainly not be willing to examine the goal itself.

The attempts at "self-analysis" made by Simon Fenimore in Somerset Maugham's *Christmas Holiday* exemplify this kind of approach. It is Simon's driving life ambition to attain a huge vindictive triumph over others. He analyzes and changes in himself those qualities that might deflect him from his role as the future Gestapo chief in a totalitarian state and in the same manner he singles out and develops those tendencies which will enable him to become more efficient and destructive. With such a goal in mind he could not possibly be interested in analyzing his incapacity for love, his asceticism, or his cynicism. Similarly a woman who believes in "love" as the magic solution to all her distress could not possibly touch upon her hidden aggressiveness, her morbid dependency, or her lack of resourcefulness. She would analyze in herself only those factors that render it more

238

difficult for her to find or to attach to herself a man who would fulfill her magic expectations. In other words the patient must have abandoned his neurotic goals or at least have questioned their validity.

Secondly, the patient must have his feet sufficiently on the ground; he must be interested in seeing himself as he *is* and *could be* instead of trying to live up to a phantastic notion of what he should be or of seeing himself merely as the superior being he is in his imagination.

Finally, the patient must have gained sufficient incentive to continue working with himself; he must have overcome the pervasive feeling of hopelessness and the paralyzing inertia resulting from it, expressed by the "I can't" attitude. He must have largely overcome his tendency to make others responsible for his difficulties, and he must realize instead that heaven and hell are within himself.

Is it possible, then, to estimate in analysis when these conditions are fulfilled? I believe that one can be fairly accurate about the time when the patient is no longer obsessed by neurotic goals. The two other conditions, being more comprehensive, are more difficult to gauge. The following criteria would be important. Does the patient have a more spontaneous interest in facing his problems and working at them? Has he become more capable of observing and understanding himself outside the analytic sessions? Has he become more honest with himself? Has he become more co-operative in his relations with the analyst?

239

But in spite of such criteria the evaluation will remain tentative. And the analysis should be terminated with a clear understanding of the tentative nature of the step. While the patient should be prepared to work by himself and to try to find the solutions to his problems without leaning on the analyst at every opportunity, he should, nevertheless, feel secure in the knowledge that he can always discuss matters with his analyst should any problem prove too difficult for him.

How are you to proceed from here? You go on examining yourself; if a difficulty arises, you try to recognize your share in it; you learn from experience; in short you analyze yourself. I need not delve here into the polemics concerning the possibility, feasibility, and limitations of self-analysis. Though it has not yet been determined how many people can analyze themselves successfully and to what extent they can do it without previous treatment, there is no doubt whatever that self-analysis is feasible after analytical treatment.

It would not be appropriate within the framework of this book to discuss at length the procedure of self-analysis. I prefer, therefore, to present an example which will illustrate some of the most important points. My illustration will demonstrate that self-analysis, far from being superficial, can penetrate to deeply repressed neurotic drives, if we are sufficiently bent on finding the truth about ourselves. It will also show that what counts in the procedure is our attitude and the spirit in which we go about it.

The example is presented in very condensed form—it omits many minor difficulties and abortive erroneous pursuits and points out only the highlights in a piece of self-analysis extending over a period of nine months. Although I have tried to present it as simply as possible, it may be difficult for you to understand the amount of work done and to follow its sequence because it touches upon problems with which you may not be familiar. But for more than one reason it may be worth your while not only to read it but to make a thorough study of it. It constitutes a particularly successful piece of self-analysis on the part of an interior decorator, Eileen, who had gone through a short but rather successful analysis some years earlier. Certain inhibitions in her work and an overdependent attitude toward her husband had greatly diminished.

Before Eileen arrived at the stage of self-analysis presented here, she had already recognized to what an extent she was glorifying her appeasing, conciliatory attitude. Although she had known for a long time that these trends were mostly conditioned by fears, she had nevertheless registered them at their face value and unconsciously credited herself with being an unusually good person. This "halosickness" as she herself called it had been very much under cover and it had taken her a long time to unearth it.

Eileen, then, began to investigate her "putting up

with too much." She found that she was tolerating fairly flagrant impositions and insults. In many instances she was not even aware of being unfairly treated or became aware of it only much later. Instead she would react to the offender with an increase of appeasing endeavor. She had noticed this weakness before, but could not approach it realistically until the analysis of her "halo-sickness" had dispelled much of her eagerness to appear better than she was.

She now observed many isolated instances in which she was putting up with such impositions, and this led her to the discovery that she actually reacted to such occurrences with rage. This rage had hitherto been hidden under spells of paralyzing fatigue. Her reactions still remained delayed for some time. She would wake up in the middle of the night enraged at someone by whom she had felt badly treated. She had done that before but she could now connect her anger reaction with specific situations in which she had been insulted, imposed upon, or disregarded. She also discovered that she had no such reactions whenever she had been able to assert herself.

She then discovered that her anger was directed not only against the offender but even more against herself. She arrived at a clearer understanding of the nature of her anger when she observed a change in her attitude toward "nice" people. Formerly she had tended to like them indiscriminately; now she became more and more alert to their appeasing strategies and would designate them in her mind as "doormats," thus expressing her contempt for their cringing attitude. In this roundabout way she became aware of the angry contempt she had for her own cringing.

Eileen now began to wonder why her anger reactions were so intense. She observed that their intensity was usually not warranted by the occasion. Comparatively trivial matters upset her greatly. An unappreciative or overly demanding customer, an impolite taxi driver might throw her completely out of gear. This observation was disturbing, because it undermined rationalizations and pointed to an unknown disorder within her. Was there an explosive force powerful enough to be touched off by the slightest provocation? At the same time the realization was promising because it aroused her interest to find out about the nature of these unconscious forces.

For months she tried in vain to find an answer. She asked herself whether she was not perhaps more aggressive than she believed; whether she was actually motivated by a desire to triumph over others and felt disgracefully defeated whenever she could not even defend herself. These were very sensible questions but they did not strike the right chord in her; they remained speculative and theoretical. Perhaps she tried to solve the problem too directly or too intellectually, instead of simply continuing to observe herself. To call this a period of resistance would be misleading. Actually another problem had to be tackled before this one could become accessible.

I dwell on this uneventful period because temporary

impasses like this one are bound to occur in every analysis and may easily lead to feelings of discouragement unless it is kept in mind that one cannot unlock the suitcase in a closet without first unlocking the closet.

An accidental experience finally supplied the missing link. Eileen fractured her leg in an automobile accident. Since no private rooms were available in the hospital, she was placed in the general ward. At first she felt this to be quite unbearable and verged on despair. She urged her husband repeatedly to obtain a private room for her. Then the thought flashed through her mind: "Maybe some patient who has a private room will die and I can move into her room." Just for a flicker of a moment this thought startled her; for a flicker of a moment she realized dimly that she was reacting disproportionately to the situation and that there was violent anger behind her despair. Apparently she was not yet quite ready to grasp the meaning of this thought, but it showed that something was working in her and probably prepared the way for the insight she arrived at two days later.

By then she had overcome the first shock. She had grown familiar with the other patients and their suffering. It was then that she asked herself: "Why should I insist on being better off than these people?" And shortly thereafter a more precise question emerged: "Is there something in me that makes me feel entitled to special privileges?" The thought came to her with the utmost surprise because she had always considered herself the very opposite of demanding and arrogant. But now she was too keenly aware of it to push it aside. She realized,

244

then, that she had always felt entitled to special consideration and attention and that initial despair grew not so much from the fact that she had to lie in a ward but rather from the frustration of her claims. The annoyance she had felt at first had actually had the character of indignation—indignation at being exposed to what she felt was improper treatment.

With this insight her irritation vanished; she became patient, friendly with the others, and even began to like life in the ward. The insight opened up a vast field of hidden naïve expectations. She discovered that she had always felt entitled to good luck and favorable circumstances: timetables should be convenient; her sarcastic remarks should be taken in good grace; the weather should be fair when she went on an excursion; and so forth. Furthermore, she had always harbored the secret belief that she would never age or die. Now for the first time in her life she could think calmly and realistically that some day she would die, like everybody else.

Her relief was so profound that she believed—for a while—that she had already solved the whole problem of special claims. Actually, a great deal of work remained to be done. Nevertheless this first reaction was by no means altogether unjustified. In the first place she had managed to penetrate to a problem which for her apparently was crucial and which had been deeply repressed. For in her actual behavior she had been leaning over backwards to please others, she had been overappreciative, contented with little and had seen the wishes and rights of others much more clearly than her own. In the second place she had actually dispensed with the special claims that were involved in this particular situation. The illusory part of Eileen's reaction was the belief that the whole problem was solved for good and all.

Such illusions sometimes occur in analysis. They can be tenacious and may then present an obstacle to further progress. It may possibly have delayed progress in Eileen's case, too, but the fact is that she resumed working at the problem in subsequent months. We could make light of the reaction by saying that everybody would overrate an important finding in his first joy of discovery. But the reason I make these remarks at all is to point to a more powerful factor. As so many patients do in similar situations, Eileen indulged in wishful thinking. She would have liked to be rid of her disturbing claims without having to make the necessary effort to eradicate them.

Because she was in such a hurry to settle her problem of special claims, Eileen missed out on one important detail—namely, the flash of hope that somebody would die so that she would have the benefit of privacy. This would have revealed a certain callous aspect of her personality of which she was totally unaware. It would have been of special importance in this connection if she had reconsidered this momentary hope after she had gained insight into her special claims, for it might have revealed to her the intensity of the claims and their absolute egocentricity.

Eileen's taste of freedom during this period, short-lived as it was, nevertheless had its great value. In all likelihood it gave her an additional incentive to resume work on the problem of special claims. For she knew now, with an inner certainty that only experience can provide, that her work would be rewarded.

As she resumed her ordinary routine of life in subsequent weeks, she came up against some of her old difficulties. Each time this happened, she re-examined her special claims and thus gradually gained new insights. She came to understand more about the nature of her claims. The claims she had noticed while at the hospital concerned outside circumstances. Now she discovered additional ones of a different type: she felt entitled to special consideration, to being singled out, to being exempt from criticism and from doing what others expected of her.

Since none of these claims had ever been felt consciously or asserted openly she could discover them only in indirect ways. She realized that she sometimes felt greatly abused only to find a day or two later that the situation was but half as bad. After observing this sequence several times she arrived at the only possible conclusion, namely, that her initial reactions were exaggerated. Gradually she grew skeptical toward them. Finally she was able to question the validity of her reaction in the midst of feeling profoundly abused.

This was a difficult and, if I may say so, a brave step to take. For while she was feeling abused, her reaction seemed absolutely real to her and, hence, absolutely justified and logical considering the monumental wrong done to her. To question her own reaction, despite the

247

seemingly overwhelming evidence that she was in the right, was by no means easy but it was rewarding: she was now able to understand that her excessive reaction resulted from the frustration of her special claims.

Actually, although Eileen was not yet aware of it, this piece of analysis undermined her whole "putting up with too much" complex. She had seen before that her own compliance made her defenseless, that she hated others for being aggressive and herself for being compliant. This proved to be a true but incomplete observation. What she had not seen and actually could not see before tackling her unconscious claims for special privileges was that she overreacted to "aggression" and that the intensity of her ensuing anger was largely due to her humiliation at having her claims punctured.

Eileen also came to understand more clearly how she had rationalized her claims. These had appeared under harmless and rational screens. For instance, she had felt entitled to help from others because of her own helplessness; she had made demands on others under the guise of "love"; she had consistently dodged responsibilities toward others because she had so little time or was overworked.

A short comment on this latter piece of analysis: it was correct but it lacked depth. Only later, following the segment of analysis described here, did Eileen begin to realize the full implication of these findings. By resorting to helplessness and a lovable appearance she was persistently putting a check upon her resourcefulness and her inner independence and thereby undermining her self-confidence. Moreover, this attitude made her dependent on others and forced her into being compliant and ready to play up to others. Most important, by resorting to helplessness and lovability she actually entangled herself in an irreconcilable conflict. For although she felt entitled, unconsciously, to all sorts of special privileges, she actually got very few of them and had to ingratiate herself with people for what little she did get —thus the source of gnawing humiliation was constantly renewed. This was really the main conflict underlying the whole complex of "putting up with too much."

Eileen herself did not see these implications at the time because the appeal she could make to others on the basis of helplessness and "love" was too important to her as an implement with which to assert her claims in a hidden, indirect way. Nor was she yet ready either to relinquish her claims or to assert them in other ways.

Also she had by now lost sight of the problem of "putting up with too much." She did return to it, though, with her next finding which concerned one of her main claims. Briefly, she realized that she expected others to give her everything she felt entitled to without having to assert herself, to express a wish or even to be clear in her own mind what she wanted. Merely by appearing "nice" or friendly she would be entitled to everything. Accommodating and appeasing techniques had thus acquired an almost magic power. She now saw that her lack of assertiveness had compelled her to develop this particular claim. And she made an even more pertinent discovery, namely, that this claim, once established, actually perpetuated her weakness. A kind of magic gesture would make any self-assertion on her part unnecessary. It was even beneath her dignity to assert herself or to fight for or against anything. This, by the way, was the reason why, despite her endeavors, she had not been able to get at her aggressive trends. As long as she felt that even the most legitimate kind of aggression was undesirable, she could not possibly be interested in unearthing whatever aggressive tendencies she had. She saw how her claim for special consideration actually resulted in her "putting up with too much." She also found a more complete explanation for the intensity of the ensuing anger. It was not only anger at her own weakness—as she had originally assumed—but also an expression of feeling frustrated in her special claim.

This last insight revealed her "putting up with too much" in a new light. We can see here how, despite honest self-scrutiny, it is sometimes impossible to give an accurate description of a particular disturbance. Hitherto, Eileen had thought of her "putting up with too much" only in connection with instances in which she really was taken advantage of or unduly disregarded. Now she saw that she had not only exaggerated in her own mind the wrong done to her but that she had often reacted similarly to situations in which she was not wronged at all. These were situations in which people failed to live up to her unrealistic demands.

250

Let me summarize the segment of analysis just reported. Essentially it concerned Eileen's unassertiveness. She had first seen how glorification of her existing core of weakness gave her the illusion of being purely good-natured. When analysis undermined her unconscious pretenses of "goodness," she was able to face her unassertiveness directly. She reacted to this realization with violent anger at others and at herself but felt unable to change. Strangely enough she made no real efforts to become more assertive in her everyday life, although she smarted under her compliance. And here she made her crucial discovery, namely that her desire to become stronger was paralyzed by her unconscious feeling of being entitled to a soft and easy life. Others should guess her wishes, should help her, yield to her, and fight her little battles without any effort at assertion on her part. Naturally, this bit of expected magic did not work. Time and again she was merely confronted with reality. Only after she had recognized and relinquished her special claims could she feel free to make efforts in her own behalf.

Such discoveries are not arrived at easily. On the contrary, I can assure you from experience that they are extremely difficult to make even with the help of an analyst. It is true that many questions were left unanswered. Eileen had yet to discover many of the roots of her special claims on life and to find out why they had been so deeply repressed. But it is true of any piece of thorough analysis that, as some problems are satisfactorily solved, others begin to be discernible. Eileen's was a real achievement and her success has greatly strengthened my confidence in the amount of analytical work that can be done alone.

What made it possible for this patient to attain such comparatively good results? Or, in other words, how can Eileen's experiences benefit your efforts at self-analysis?

Eileen's quiet determination to recognize and go to the roots of the factors in herself that blocked her way was of paramount importance. Her determination was apparent in the consistency of her efforts. You may protest here that there was no system in her attempts, that in fact they appear to have been quite sporadic, that months passed between one trial at self-analysis and another, months in which nothing apparently happened. True enough. But I am sure that even during this time more must have gone on in Eileen's mind than she reported or was aware of.

Certainly there was no regularity of conscious effort in the sense that she set apart an hour every day in which to analyze herself. When I spoke of her consistent determination to reach a certain goal, I was not thinking of a regular working schedule. I am not in favor of such planned regularity. Self-analysis pursued in this manner can too easily become an aim in itself—art for art's sake —instead of a living struggle with concrete difficulties. Besides, the resolution to analyze oneself day by day at a fixed time cannot be carried out anyway. External matters may interfere or you may not be in the proper frame of mind. Your intentions will easily peter out or your resolution to analyze yourself will become an inner obligation which you stick to under duress. As a result your work is in danger of turning sterile because you are likely to feel it as a self-imposed yoke and revolt against it. If, on the other hand, you analyze yourself when you really feel like doing so, your incentive will be fresh and spontaneous.

If you analyze your difficulties as they arise, you will gladly turn to analysis as you might turn to a friend when you are in distress. This is exactly what Eileen did. She tackled her problems whenever she felt in need of clarification, and she pursued them as far as she could each time. Only once—when she actually reached an impasse—did she try to force a solution, but in so doing, accomplished nothing. Then her problem would seemingly lie dormant for a time. But when another difficult situation arose or when she was caught once more in the grip of neurotic disturbances, her energies were mobilized and she would make another attempt at understanding her difficulties.

Eileen's consistent determination to come to grips with herself expressed itself in another way as well: she never grew discouraged. Even when she came to an impasse while analyzing her "putting up with too much" attitude, she did not show any marked signs of despair or impatience. Rather, she let the problem lie dormant until a new approach to it opened up. She did not expect miracles; she was fully aware that analysis is a slow process. But she also knew that every finding would contribute to an eventual solution even though it might not yield immediate tangible results. Recall the time when she believed that her entire problem was now solved. Even when she understood that this belief had been partly illusory, she was not discouraged. She simply realized that more work remained to be done.

A further way in which Eileen expressed her consistent determination has already been touched on. What Eileen actually tackled from various angles throughout the whole period described was her feeling of being abused by others. You have probably experienced such a feeling and know therefore how tempting it is to immerse yourself in it and respond with self-pity or rage against others. Before her analytical treatment, Eileen, too, had had profound spells of despairing self-pity. During this period of self-analysis, however, her temptations to deal with the problem through rage or self-pity were but short-lived. Time and again we see her going straight to the point of searching for her own share in the difficulty.

You may still expect me to discuss technical details regarding self-analysis. But remember that I am not dealing here with self-analysis in general but with the more specific subject of self-analysis following analytical treatment. When you have been analyzed you will be familiar with the fundamentals of the procedure. Moreover, just as every patient behaves differently in analysis, so each one will evolve his particular ways of analyzing himself. As I gather from inquiries concerning self-analysis, many people seem to harbor the illusion that technical rules would supply them with a magic key opening the gates to self-recognition. What is of crucial importance, however, in analysis as elsewhere, is the spirit in which it is done.

What were the practical results of Eileen's self-analysis during the period outlined above? To begin with, a disturbing symptom disappeared: the spells of fatigue, which had already diminished as a result of previous analytical work, now vanished for good and all. She became less tense in her relations with others; she felt less easily abused and whenever feelings of impotent rage at being "victimized" did emerge, she was quick to detect them and could then deal with the particular situation in a more sober and matter-of-fact way. She became more discriminating toward others. Since her expectations had become less exorbitant and undercurrents of hostility had diminished, she could see other people more realistically than before. She was also able to participate more spontaneously in discussions at professional as well as social gatherings. Formerly she had felt like a bystander; her efforts to contribute her share had, at best, been strained. This latter change may seem insignificant but I regard it as an evidence that Eileen felt less apart from others. Since she felt less unique in a fictitious way she was able to enter into closer relations with others.

At the same time she felt more capable of defending herself whenever necessary, of expressing her own wishes and opinions and standing up for them. In other words, she felt less "chosen by God" and could thus be more of a real person.

I have described the results of this segment of analysis in such detail because it permits of a generalization. Of course not every piece of analysis will result in the disappearance of a symptom—as in this case the remnants of neurotic fatigue. Moreover, the nature of the symptom that does diminish or disappear varies from case to case. But the more subtle character changes resulting from the thorough analysis of any problem are essentially similar. Supposing, for example, that the problem concerned a person's insatiable hunger for success and triumph, analysis of this entirely different situation would similarly result in a diminution of vulnerability and isolation.

In the light of absolute achievement, the practical results of any piece of analysis are not at all impressive. "What is the use of making all these efforts toward self-recognition," you may say, "if they result each time merely in a little less of this and a little more of that?" Is not analysis, then, an endless road toward a destination it never reaches? True. And because it is true we had better face it. But this outlook is discouraging only as long as we are captivated by the vision of absolute and ultimate attainment.

It is certainly necessary to be aware of our goals lest we flounder aimlessly. But what really matters is the actual process of living and the actual steps we take toward our goals. Whether we take these steps alone or with the help of an analyst, the result each time is a gain in inner strength and freedom.